50 TIPS & TRICKS FOR THE NEW DYNAMICS AX

Rev 1 – RTW Release

Murray Fife

ISBN-13: 978-1522902119

ISBN-10: 1522902112

Preface

What You Need for This Guide

All the examples shown in this guide were done with the New Microsoft Dynamics AX virtual machine image that was downloaded from the Microsoft CustomerSource or PartnerSource site. If you don't have your own installation of New Microsoft Dynamics AX, you can also use the images found on the Microsoft Learning Download Center or deployed through Lifecycle Services. The following list of software from the virtual image was leveraged within this guide:

> Microsoft Dynamics AX

Even though all the preceding software was used during the development and testing of the recipes in this book, they may also work on earlier versions of the software with minor tweaks and adjustments, and should also work on later versions without any changes.

Errata

Although we have taken every care to ensure the accuracy of our content, mistakes do happen. If you find a mistake in one of our books—maybe a mistake in the text or the code—we would be grateful if you would report this to us. By doing so, you can save other readers from frustration and help us improve subsequent versions of this book. If you find any errata, please report them by emailing editor@blindsquirrelpublishing.com.

Piracy

Piracy of copyright material on the Internet is an ongoing problem across all media. If you come across any illegal copies of our works, in any form, on the Internet, please provide us with the location address or website name immediately so that we can pursue a remedy.

Please contact us at legal@blindsquirrelpublishing.com with a link to the suspected pirated material.

We appreciate your help in protecting our authors, and our ability to bring you valuable content.

Questions

You can contact us at help@blindsquirrelpublishing.com if you are having a problem with any aspect of the book, and we will do our best to address it.

Table of Contents

INTRODUCTION...7

Using Workspaces..9

Workspace tiles..13

Workspace favorites lists..17

Switching favorites lists..19

Drilling into details through hyperlinks..21

Document detail forms..25

Expanding the fast tabs...27

Toggling Between The Header and Lines View...31

Using the dropdown menus...35

Pinning the Navigation Menu 39

Unpinning the Navigation Menu...43

Accessing the workspaces through the menu 47

Using the employee self service workspace 51

The system administrator workspace..59

Accessing Lifecycle Services 63

Using the search to find functions 71

USING LIST PAGES 75

Showing the fact boxes..77

Accessing detail forms 81

Accessing the ribbon bar commands...85

Collapsing the Ribbon Bar...89

Undocking forms..95

Using the list filter...101

Zooming 107

PERSONALIZATION 111

Hiding fields 113

Unhiding fields 119

Adding additional fields 127

Moving fields 137

Filtering lists 145

Saving user personalization 151

Importing custom views into other users 159

Using filter panel 167

Adding additional filter fields 173

Using the advanced filter 181

Adding A Filter To A Workspace As A Tile 193

Adding A Tile To The Default Dashboard 203

Adding A Filter To A Workspace As A List 209

Exporting to Excel 219

The Recent list 235

Adding favorite menu items 241

Updating user options 247

Entering an order 265

Accessing the help 285

Using the Wiki help 291

Using the task guides 297

Creating your own task guides 309

Exporting task recordings to Lifecycle Services 329

Viewing task recordings in Lifecycle Services 335

Changing the default company banner image 345

Running financial reports...359

Creating demo data 371

Enabling Power BI 381

Connecting to Power BI 393

Adding Power BI tiles to workspaces..401

Creating a data export template using data management...........................407

Creating a data export 421

Downloading your data to a package 427

Importing data packages into other entities 437

CONCLUSION..453

INTRODUCTION

The new Dynamics AX is a big change from the previous releases. The majority of the changes are around the new web based user interface, the new way that you navigate around in the application and also new sets of tools that have come along for the ride.

For those of you that are familiar with the older user interfaces then you may have to learn a couple of new tricks to get around the system like the pro that you are, and for new users of the new Dynamics AX environments then you will probably want as many tips on all the cool things that you are hidden away within the application so that you can quickly become a power user of the system.

If that's the case then this is the guide for you – we have scoured all of the resources that we have to compile 50 of the most useful tips and tricks for the new Dynamics AX and that will be useful to everyone, regardless of if you are a novice to Dynamics AX just trying to get around in the application, or have worked with the previous versions of the system, and are just want to learn the nuances of the new user interface.

 www.dynamicsaxcompanions.com
Dynamics AX Companions
- 7 -
www.blindsquirrelpublishing.com
© 2015 Blind Squirrel Publishing, LLC, All Rights Reserved

Using Workspaces

The first type of page that we will see is the main dashboard view. Here you will see that there are a number of Workspaces that are available that have been tailored to specific roles within the organization.

To go to any particular workspace, then all you have to do is click on the tile.

How to do it...

For example if you were an order entry clerk then you would probably just click on the Sales Order Processing and Inquiry workspace tile.

Now you are within the Sales order processing and inquiry workspace you will be presented with all of the core information that is necessary to track all of your sales orders and also link out to the other areas that you may need to help you along the way.

Using Workspaces

How to do it...

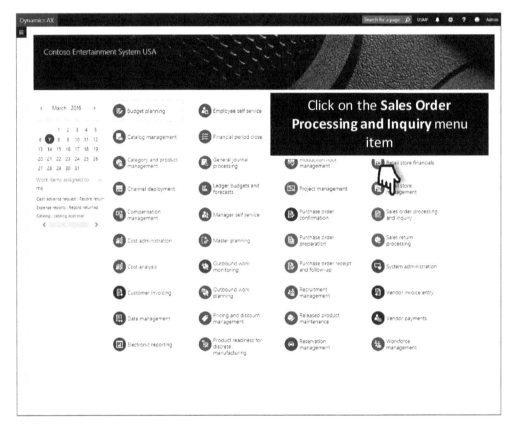

For example if you were an order entry clerk then you would probably just click on the Sales Order Processing and Inquiry workspace tile.

Using Workspaces

How to do it...

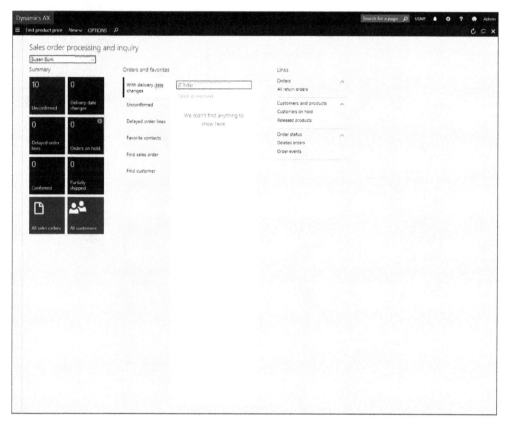

Now you are within the Sales order processing and inquiry workspace you will be presented with all of the core information that is necessary to track all of your sales orders and also link out to the other areas that you may need to help you along the way.

Workspace tiles

On the left hand side of the page you will see the workspace tiles. These are quick visuals that show you how many particular transactions are sitting within the status, and also quick links to other detail and list pages within the application.

How to do it...

For example, if you look at the Unconfirmed orders tile, we can see that there are 14 orders in that status.

If we want to see the orders themselves, then we can just click on the Unconfirmed orders tile.

This will take us straight to the list page that shows us all of the individual orders that are grouped under the tile.

daxc
www.dynamicsaxcompanions.com
Dynamics AX Companions

- 13 -

www.blindsquirrelpublishing.com
© 2015 Blind Squirrel Publishing, LLC , All Rights Reserved

 BLIND SQUIRREL PUBLISHING

Workspace tiles

How to do it…

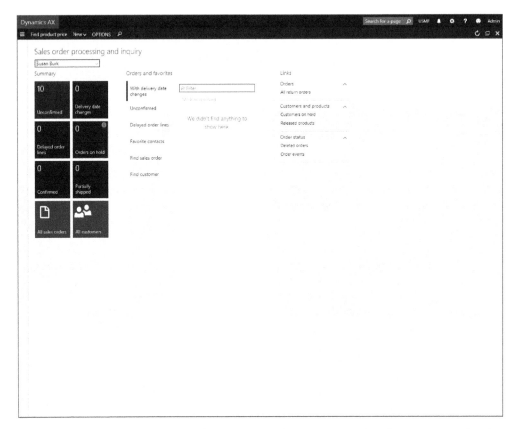

For example, if you look at the Unconfirmed orders tile, we can see that there are 14 orders in that status.

dαxc   www.dynamicsaxcompanions.com
Dynamics AX Companions
- 14 -
www.blindsquirrelpublishing.com
© 2015 Blind Squirrel Publishing, LLC , All Rights Reserved
BLIND SQUIRREL
PUBLISHING

Workspace tiles

How to do it...

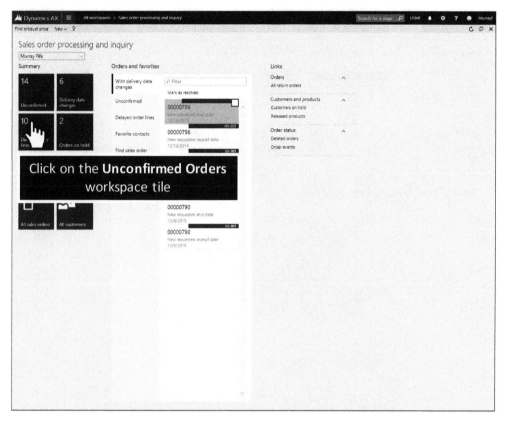

If we want to see the orders themselves, then we can just click on the Unconfirmed orders tile.

da⌀c   www.dynamicsaxcompanions.com
Dynamics AX Companions

www.blindsquirrelpublishing.com
© 2015 Blind Squirrel Publishing, LLC , All Rights Reserved

BLIND SQUIRREL
PUBLISHING

Workspace tiles

How to do it…

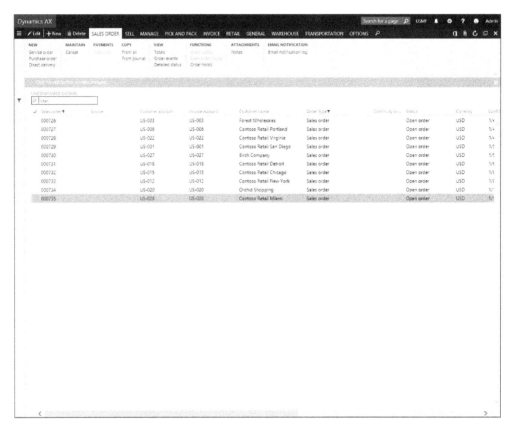

This will take us straight to the list page that shows us all of the individual orders that are grouped under the tile.

Workspace favorites lists

In the center of the form you will see an area where you can see more links to documents and transactions that should be important for your job.

How to do it...

These favorites lists are quick ways to open up records that you need to work on without having to navigate to other forms within the system.

daxc   www.dynamicsaxcompanions.com
Dynamics AX Companions

- 17 -

www.blindsquirrelpublishing.com
© 2015 Blind Squirrel Publishing, LLC , All Rights Reserved
 BLIND SQUIRREL
PUBLISHING

Workspace favorites lists

How to do it...

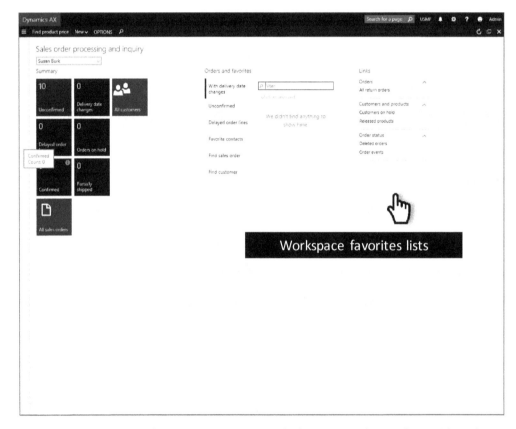

These favorites lists are quick ways to open up records that you need to work on without having to navigate to other forms within the system.

Switching favorites lists

You will notice that there are a number of different favorites listed in this example, and as you switch between them you will be able to see different groups of data, and also some of the data has different data.

How to do it...

For example, if you click on the Unconfirmed tab then you will see anther way to track all of the unconfirmed orders.

Switching favorites lists

How to do it…

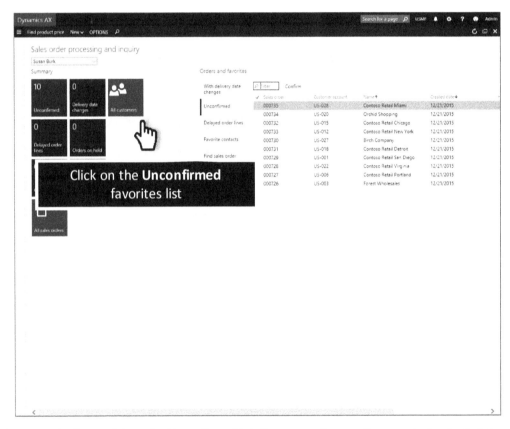

For example, if you click on the Unconfirmed tab then you will see anther way to track all of the unconfirmed orders.

Drilling into details through hyperlinks

If you need to view any of the detailed information for the transaction or document that you are looking at then all you need to do is click on the hyperlink for the transaction.

How to do it...

For example, if you want to see the order 00000797, then just click on it.

This will take you straight into the detail form showing you all of the sales order lines.

Drilling into details through hyperlinks

How to do it…

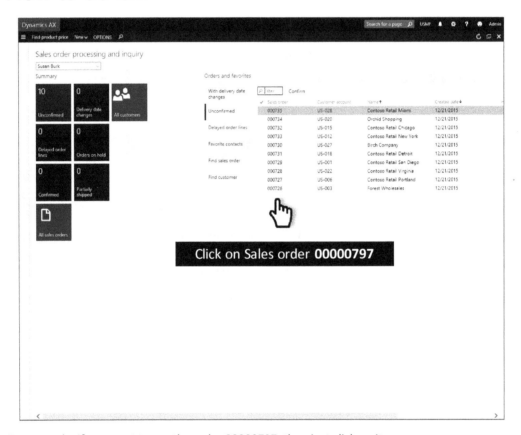

For example, if you want to see the order 00000797, then just click on it.

Drilling into details through hyperlinks

How to do it…

This will take you straight into the detail form showing you all of the sales order lines.

Document detail forms

Now that we are looking at the document record we are in the Document detail view. This view is different from the list views that we have been seeing so far because you have multiple groups of data that may be hidden as compressed Fast tabs.

How to do it...

In this example we are seeing the order lines, but also there is a fast tab that contains all of the order header details.

Document detail forms

How to do it…

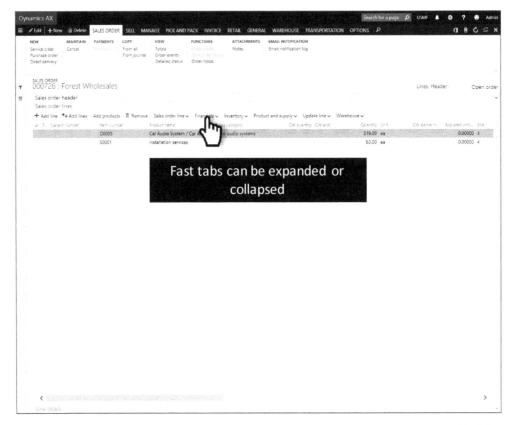

In this example we are seeing the order lines, but also there is a fast tab that contains all of the order header details.

daxc   www.dynamicsaxcompanions.com
        Dynamics AX Companions

- 26 -

www.blindsquirrelpublishing.com
© 2015 Blind Squirrel Publishing, LLC , All Rights Reserved

BLIND SQUIRREL
PUBLISHING

Expanding the fast tabs

Fast tabs are really useful because they allow you to pick and choose which sets of data that you want to see and also hide away the data that you don't necessarily need on a daily basis.

How to do it...

If you want to expand (or collapse) any of the fast tabs then all you need to do is click on the expand/collapse arrow which is at the top of each fast tab ion the right hand side.

This will expand out the fast tab and you will be able to see all of the fields that were hidden away from you.

www.dynamicsaxcompanions.com
Dynamics AX Companions

- 27 -

www.blindsquirrelpublishing.com
© 2015 Blind Squirrel Publishing, LLC , All Rights Reserved

BLIND SQUIRREL
PUBLISHING

Expanding the fast tabs

How to do it...

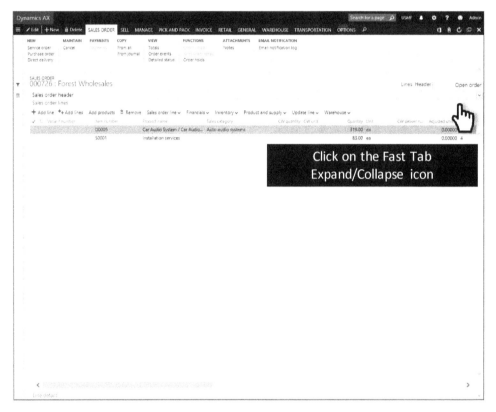

If you want to expand (or collapse) any of the fast tabs then all you need to do is click on the expand/collapse arrow which is at the top of each fast tab ion the right hand side.

Expanding the fast tabs

How to do it...

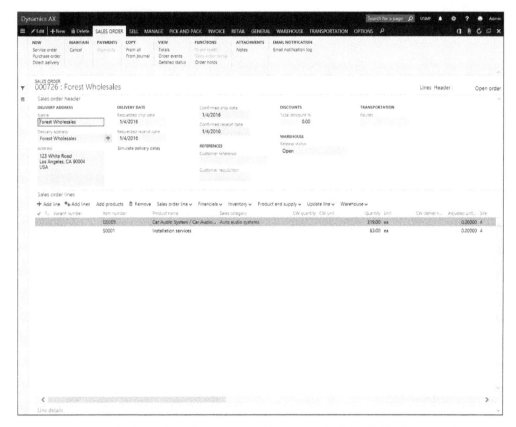

This will expand out the fast tab and you will be able to see all of the fields that were hidden away from you.

Toggling Between The Header and Lines View

One feature that has been added to make things a little bit easier for the users is the option to stitch between the Header and Line view on the forms directly on the form. For anyone who has to switch to the detail within the forms like the Sales Orders, this is a great shortcut to take advantage of.

How to do it...

To switch from the Lines view to the Header view, just click on the Header link in the title bar.

That will take you straight over to the Header view. If you want to switch back to the lines, then just click on the Lines link.

Now you are back to where you started. That was easy.

Toggling Between The Header and Lines View

How to do it…

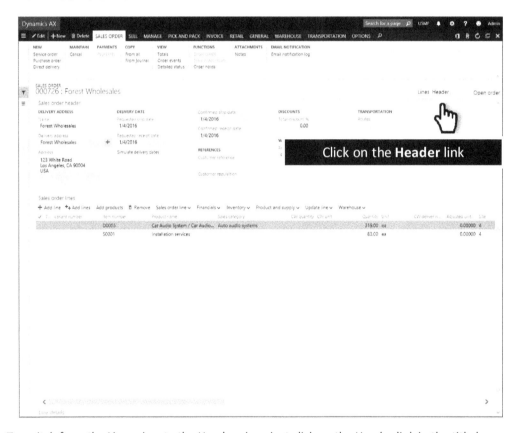

To switch from the Lines view to the Header view, just click on the Header link in the title bar.

Toggling Between The Header and Lines View

How to do it...

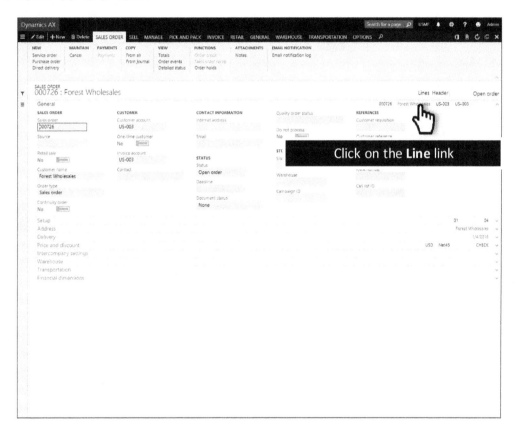

That will take you straight over to the Header view. If you want to switch back to the lines, then just click on the Lines link.

Toggling Between The Header and Lines View

How to do it…

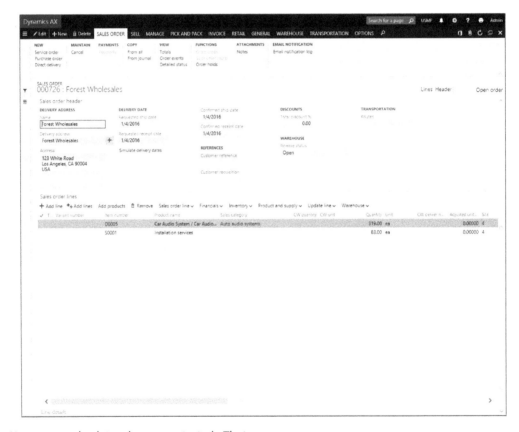

Now you are back to where you started. That was easy.

Using the dropdown menus

Another way that you can navigate through the system is through the dropdown menus. These menus allow you to access all of the different functions within the new Dynamics AX and for those that have used previous versions of AX, these are very similar in structure to the old menu pages.

How to do it...

To access the menus then just click on the hamburger icon in the top left hand corner of the application.

That will open up the Navigation Menu for you with all of the menu areas listed.

Using the dropdown menus

How to do it…

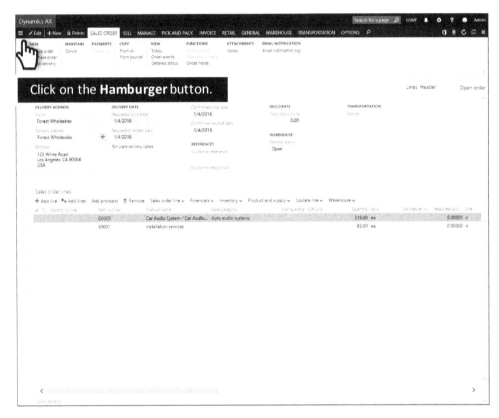

To access the menus then just click on the hamburger icon in the top left hand corner of the application.

Using the dropdown menus

How to do it…

That will open up the Navigation Menu for you with all of the menu areas listed.

Pinning the Navigation Menu

Another option that you can take advantage of with the navigation bar is to pin it to the side of the application so that you always have access to it rather than having it hidden away and accessed through the hamburger icon.

How to do it...

To do this, just click on the Pin icon on the navigation menu after you have opened it.

Now the menu bar will always stay open for you.

da⅜c www.dynamicsaxcompanions.com
Dynamics AX Companions

- 39 -

www.blindsquirrelpublishing.com
© 2015 Blind Squirrel Publishing, LLC , All Rights Reserved

 BLIND SQUIRREL
PUBLISHING

Pinning the Navigation Menu

How to do it...

To do this, just click on the Pin icon on the navigation menu after you have opened it.

daxc   www.dynamicsaxcompanions.com
       Dynamics AX Companions

- 40 -

www.blindsquirrelpublishing.com
© 2015 Blind Squirrel Publishing, LLC , All Rights Reserved

 BLIND SQUIRREL
PUBLISHING

Pinning the Navigation Menu

How to do it…

Now the menu bar will always stay open for you.

daxc www.dynamicsaxcompanions.com
Dynamics AX Companions

- 41 -

www.blindsquirrelpublishing.com
© 2015 Blind Squirrel Publishing, LLC , All Rights Reserved

BLIND SQUIRREL
PUBLISHING

Unpinning the Navigation Menu

Sometimes you may need that little bit of extra space on the screen that the menu bar is taking up when it is pinned. Don't worry, you can quickly unpin it and hide the menu at any time.

How to do it...

To do this, all you need to do is click on the << icon which was where the pin used to be.

Now the navigation menu will be hidden away from sight and you just access it by clicking on the hamburger icon.

Unpinning the Navigation Menu

How to do it…

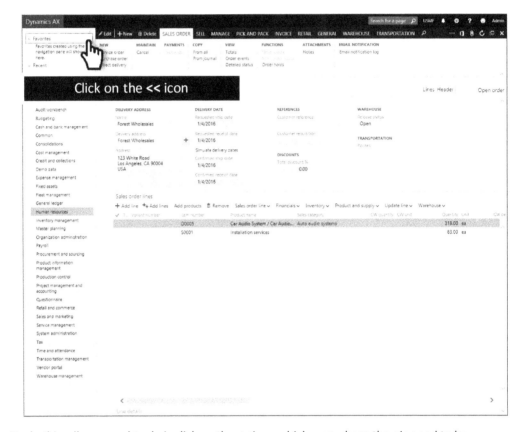

To do this, all you need to do is click on the << icon which was where the pin used to be.

Unpinning the Navigation Menu

How to do it…

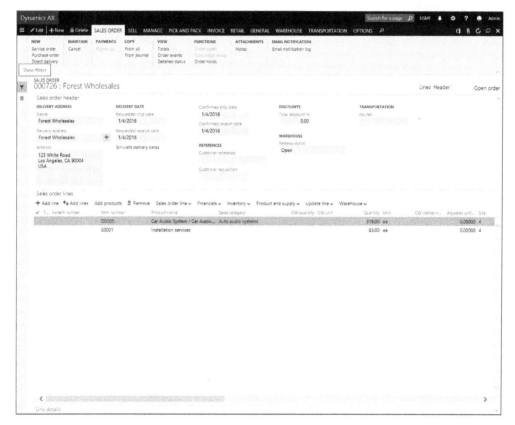

Now the navigation menu will be hidden away from sight and you just access it by clicking on the hamburger icon.

daxc   www.dynamicsaxcompanions.com
Dynamics AX Companions
www.blindsquirrelpublishing.com
© 2015 Blind Squirrel Publishing, LLC , All Rights Reserved
BLIND SQUIRREL
PUBLISHING

Accessing the workspaces through the menu

Although you can see all of the workspaces within the default dashboard that we started on, if you need to quickly open up another workspace then you can see them all through the dropdown menu.

How to do it...

For example, if you wanted to open up the Employee Self Service portal then you can find it within the workspaces sub menu, and then just click on it.

 www.dynamicsaxcompanions.com
Dynamics AX Companions

- 47 -

 www.blindsquirrelpublishing.com
© 2015 Blind Squirrel Publishing, LLC , All Rights Reserved

 BLIND SQUIRREL
PUBLISHING

Accessing the workspaces through the menu

How to do it…

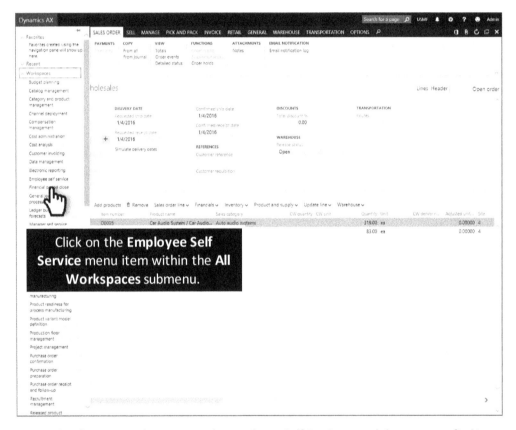

For example, if you wanted to open up the Employee Self Service portal then you can find it within the workspaces sub menu, and then just click on it.

Accessing the workspaces through the menu

How to do it…

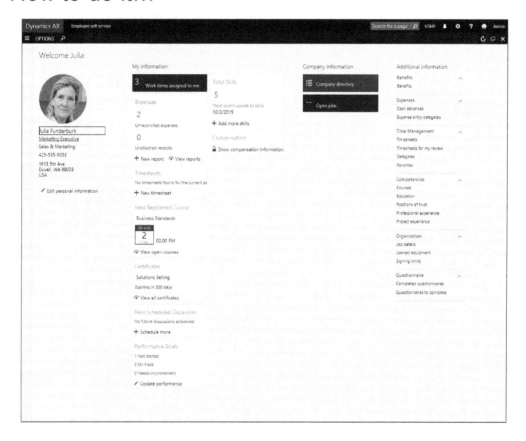

Using the employee self service workspace

The Employee Self Service workspace is an example another of the new and improved portals within the new Dynamics AX. This portal shows the employees all of their HR information which they can maintain, and also allows them to track all of their skills and competencies.

How to do it...

For example, if we wanted to edit any of our personal details from here then you just have to click on the Edit personal information link.

This will open up a form that shows all of the personal and contact information that is maintained within the application. Here you can update your address, phone number, email address, and even your own personal image that will show within the application

If you want to change the image then it's as simple as clicking on the Upload new image button.

This will allow you to find the image that you want to use within Dynamics AX and then click on the Open button to upload it.

Once you have done that, click on the x button in the top right hand corner to close out of the Personal Information form.

When you return back to the Employee self service workspace and refresh the page you will now have a new employee picture.

Using the employee self service workspace

How to do it…

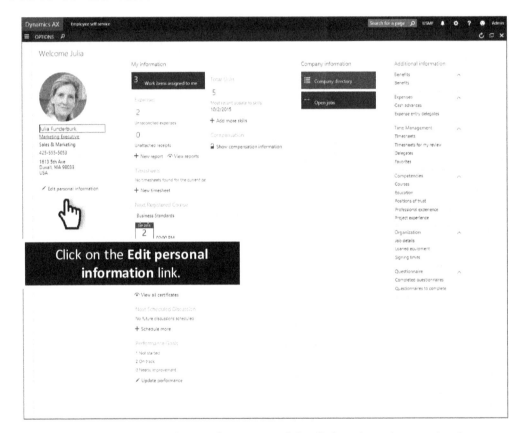

For example, if we wanted to edit any of our personal details from here then you just have to click on the Edit personal information link.

Using the employee self service workspace

How to do it…

This will open up a form that shows all of the personal and contact information that is maintained within the application. Here you can update your address, phone number, email address, and even your own personal image that will show within the application

Using the employee self service workspace

How to do it…

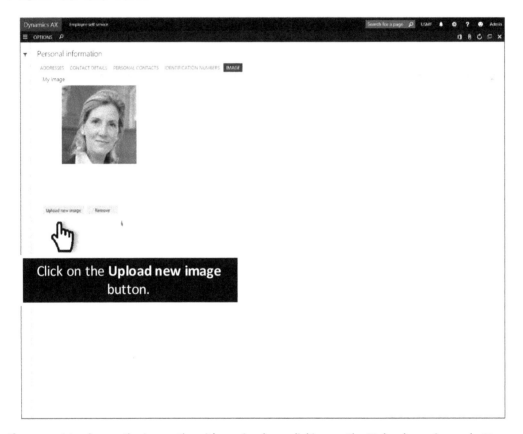

If you want to change the image then it's as simple as clicking on the Upload new image button.

Using the employee self service workspace

How to do it…

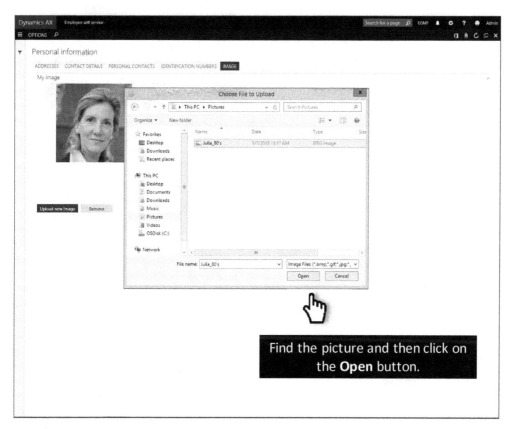

This will allow you to find the image that you want to use within Dynamics AX and then click on the Open button to upload it.

Using the employee self service workspace

How to do it…

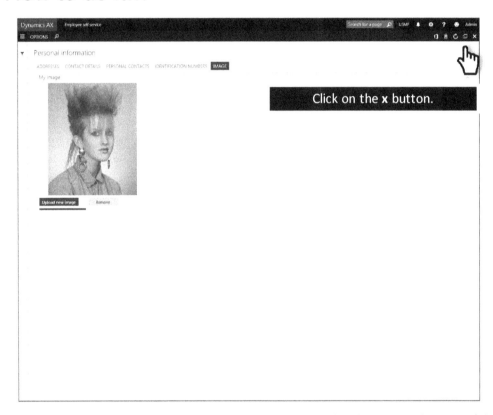

Once you have done that, click on the x button in the top right hand corner to close out of the Personal Information form.

Using the employee self service workspace

How to do it...

When you return back to the Employee self service workspace and refresh the page you will now have a new employee picture.

daxc   www.dynamicsaxcompanions.com
Dynamics AX Companions
- 57 -
www.blindsquirrelpublishing.com
© 2015 Blind Squirrel Publishing, LLC , All Rights Reserved
BLIND SQUIRREL
PUBLISHING

The system administrator workspace

Another workspace that is interesting to look at is the System administrators workspace. This is a secure workspace that allows the administrators of the application to see all of the processes that have ran, and also access other tools like Data Management, and also Lifecycle Services.

How to do it...

To access the System Administrators workspace click on the Dynamics AX link in the top right of the form to return back to the default dashboard and then click on the System administration tile.

This will open up the System administration workspace where you will be able to access some of the key tools that the System Administrator would need to use.

The system administrator workspace

How to do it…

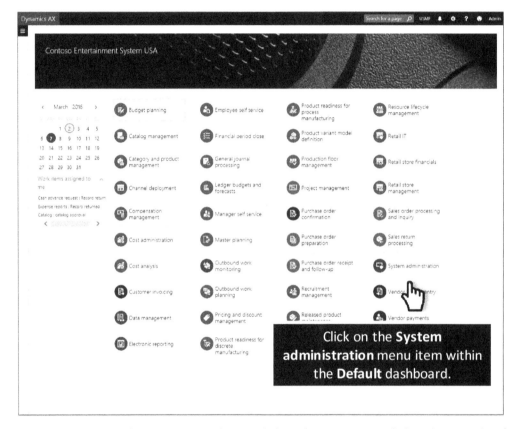

To access the System Administrators workspace click on the Dynamics AX link in the top right of the form to return back to the default dashboard and then click on the System administration tile.

The system administrator workspace

How to do it...

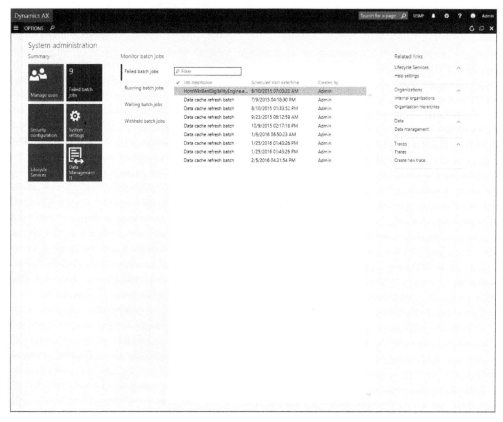

This will open up the System administration workspace where you will be able to access some of the key tools that the System Administrator would need to use.

dax www.dynamicsaxcompanions.com
Dynamics AX Companions
- 61 -
www.blindsquirrelpublishing.com
© 2015 Blind Squirrel Publishing, LLC , All Rights Reserved
BLIND SQUIRREL
PUBLISHING

Accessing Lifecycle Services

One of the tools that is highly leveraged by the new Dynamics AX is Lifecycle Services which handles a lot of the management of the project and also holds a whole slew of resources for Dynamics AX that you can take advantage of. You don't have to hunt around for the link to Lifecycle Services though – you can access it directly from the **System Administration** workspace.

How to do it...

To do this, click on the Lifecycle Services tile within the System administration workspace.

This will take you right to the Lifecycle Services project page that is associated with your Dynamics AX environment.

If you wanted to access the Business process models that you are creating throughout the project then just scroll over to the right a little and click on the Business process modeler tile.

From here you will see all of the different business process models associated with the project, and you can just click on the one that you want to browse to.

Here you will see all of the different process steps that you may have business process models associated with. You can drill into the lower levels.

You will notice that there are multiple levels here and as you drill down you will get to more and more granular business processes.

 www.dynamicsaxcompanions.com
Dynamics AX Companions

- 63 -

www.blindsquirrelpublishing.com
© 2015 Blind Squirrel Publishing, LLC , All Rights Reserved

 BLIND SQUIRREL
PUBLISHING

When you open up any of the business processes that have been documented then you will see all of the business flows and also the text narrative that describes how the process works.

Accessing Lifecycle Services

How to do it…

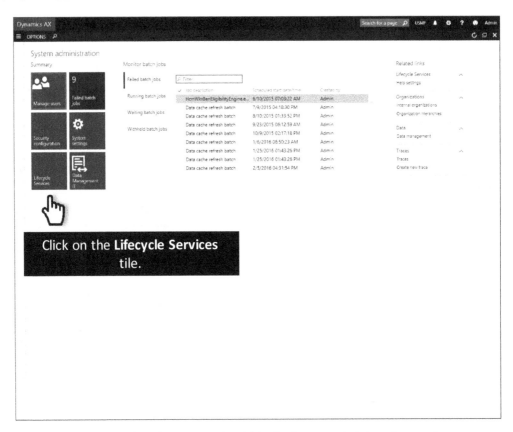

To do this, click on the Lifecycle Services tile within the System administration workspace.

daXc   www.dynamicsaxcompanions.com
Dynamics AX Companions

- 64 -

www.blindsquirrelpublishing.com
© 2015 Blind Squirrel Publishing, LLC , All Rights Reserved

BLIND SQUIRREL
PUBLISHING

Accessing Lifecycle Services

How to do it…

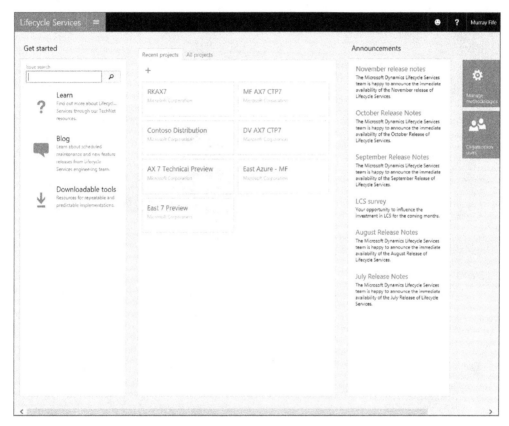

This will take you right to the Lifecycle Services project page that is associated with your Dynamics AX environment.

Accessing Lifecycle Services

How to do it...

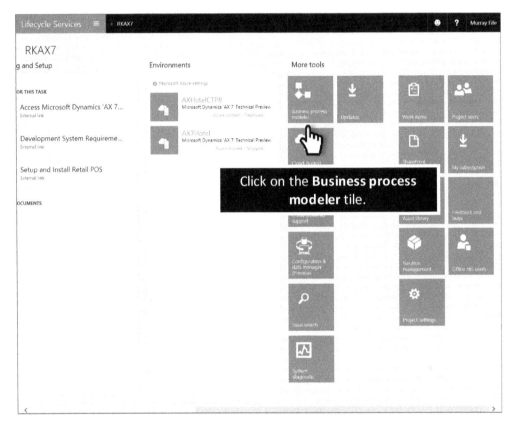

If you wanted to access the Business process models that you are creating throughout the project then just scroll over to the right a little and click on the Business process modeler tile.

daxc   www.dynamicsaxcompanions.com
Dynamics AX Companions

- 66 -

www.blindsquirrelpublishing.com
© 2015 Blind Squirrel Publishing, LLC , All Rights Reserved

BLIND SQUIRREL
PUBLISHING

Accessing Lifecycle Services

How to do it…

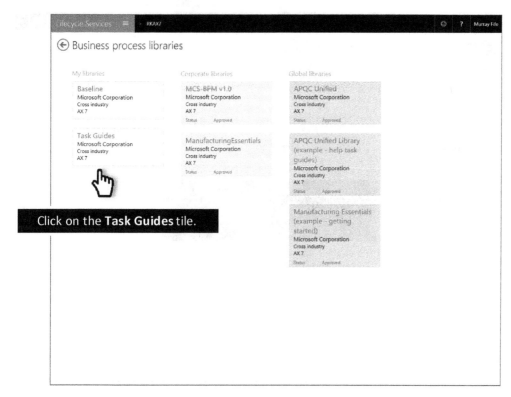

From here you will see all of the different business process models associated with the project, and you can just click on the one that you want to browse to.

daxc

www.dynamicsaxcompanions.com
Dynamics AX Companions

- 67 -

www.blindsquirrelpublishing.com
© 2015 Blind Squirrel Publishing, LLC , All Rights Reserved

BLIND SQUIRREL
PUBLISHING

Accessing Lifecycle Services

How to do it…

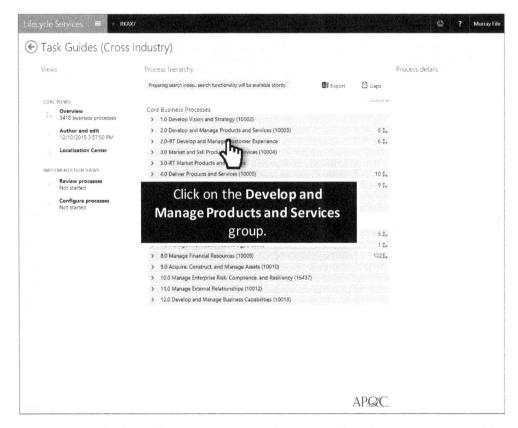

Here you will see all of the different process steps that you may have business process models associated with. You can drill into the lower levels.

daxc   www.dynamicsaxcompanions.com
Dynamics AX Companions
- 68 -
www.blindsquirrelpublishing.com
© 2015 Blind Squirrel Publishing, LLC , All Rights Reserved
BLIND SQUIRREL
PUBLISHING

Accessing Lifecycle Services

How to do it…

You will notice that there are multiple levels here and as you drill down you will get to more and more granular business processes.

Accessing Lifecycle Services

How to do it…

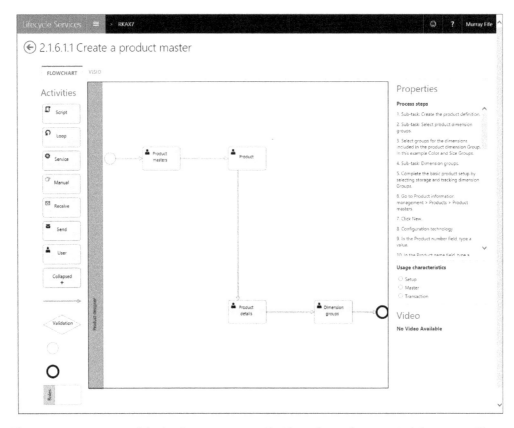

When you open up any of the business processes that have been documented then you will see all of the business flows and also the text narrative that describes how the process works.

Using the search to find functions

If you are looking for a specific form or function within Dynamics AX then you don't always need to search for it through the menu like we have been doing so far. If you know the general function that you want then you can use the search function to find it for you.

How to do it...

For example, if you wanted to find the Customers maintenance form then you can just type in all customers into the search box in the header of the application.

This will show you a list of all the functions that match your search. In this case there are a number of different ways that you can get to the Customers maintenance form, we just need to select one.

Now you will be in the All Customers list page.

Using the search to find functions

How to do it…

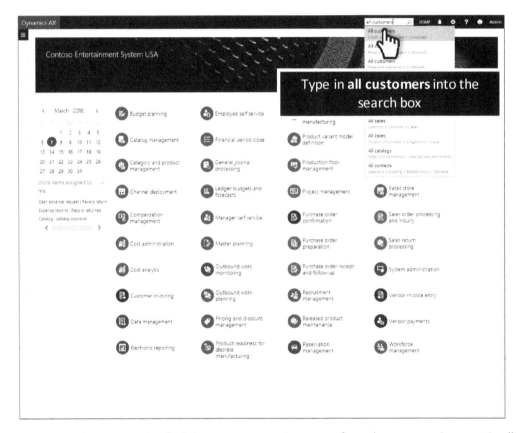

For example, if you wanted to find the Customers maintenance form then you can just type in all customers into the search box in the header of the application.

daxc www.dynamicsaxcompanions.com
Dynamics AX Companions
- 72 -
www.blindsquirrelpublishing.com
© 2015 Blind Squirrel Publishing, LLC , All Rights Reserved
BLIND SQUIRREL
PUBLISHING

Using the search to find functions

How to do it…

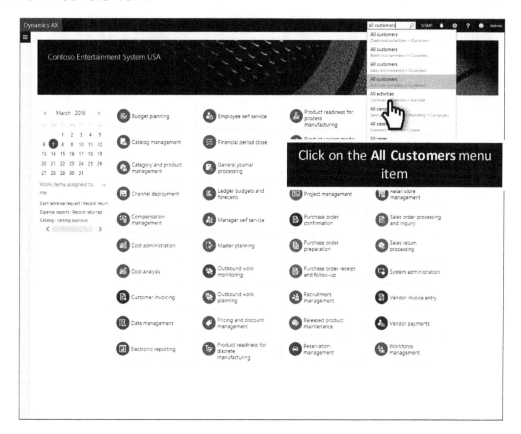

Click on the **All Customers** menu item

This will show you a list of all the functions that match your search. In this case there are a number of different ways that you can get to the Customers maintenance form, we just need to select one.

Using the search to find functions

How to do it…

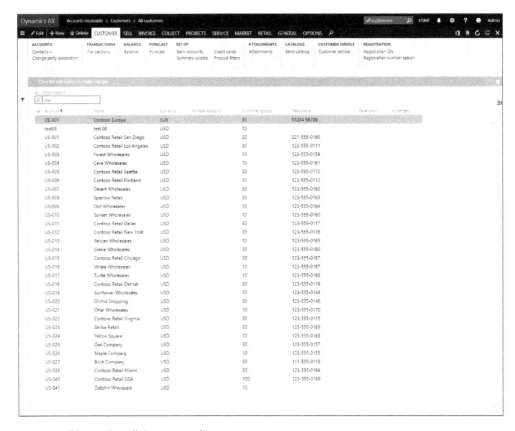

Now you will be in the All Customers list page.

daxc www.dynamicsaxcompanions.com
Dynamics AX Companions
- 74 -
www.blindsquirrelpublishing.com
© 2015 Blind Squirrel Publishing, LLC , All Rights Reserved
BLIND SQUIRREL
PUBLISHING

USING LIST PAGES

Now you will be within a list page that shows you all of the customer details. Almost all of the list pages look like this, and we will look at some of the features of the list pages that you can take advantage of.

da✗c   www.dynamicsaxcompanions.com
        Dynamics AX Companions

- 75 -

www.blindsquirrelpublishing.com
© 2015 Blind Squirrel Publishing, LLC , All Rights Reserved

BLIND SQUIRREL
PUBLISHING

Showing the fact boxes

The first thing that we will show are the Fact Boxes. These give you summary information about the record that you are in without having to open up the detail form.

How to do it...

By default these are collapsed on the right hand side of the form, but to see them all you need to do is click on the expand icon.

This will open up the Fact box panel and you will be able to see information specific to the record that you are on.

If you click on any of the other customer records then you will see that the fact boxed change to show you the details for that record.

Showing the fact boxes

How to do it…

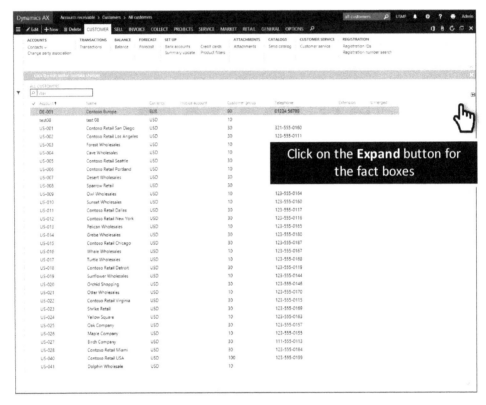

By default these are collapsed on the right hand side of the form, but to see them all you need to do is click on the expand icon.

Showing the fact boxes

How to do it…

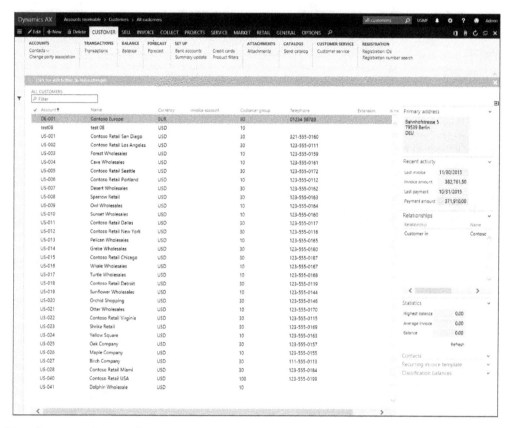

This will open up the Fact box panel and you will be able to see information specific to the record that you are on.

Showing the fact boxes

How to do it…

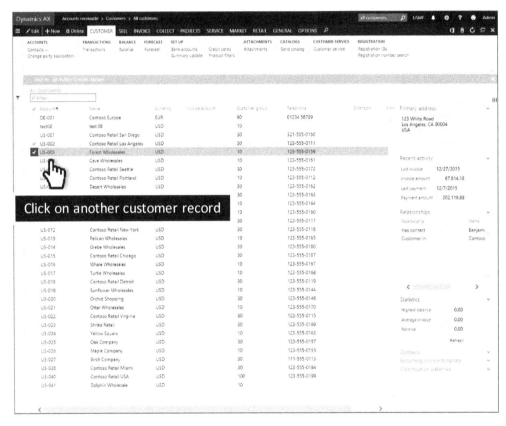

If you click on any of the other customer records then you will see that the fact boxed change to show you the details for that record.

www.dynamicsaxcompanions.com
Dynamics AX Companions

- 80 -

Accessing detail forms

From the list pages, you can also drill into the detailed information related to the record that you are looking at.

How to do it...

To do this, just click on the customer name or the customer account number.

This will open up the detailed view where you can see a lot more of the fields that are related to the record.

Accessing detail forms

How to do it…

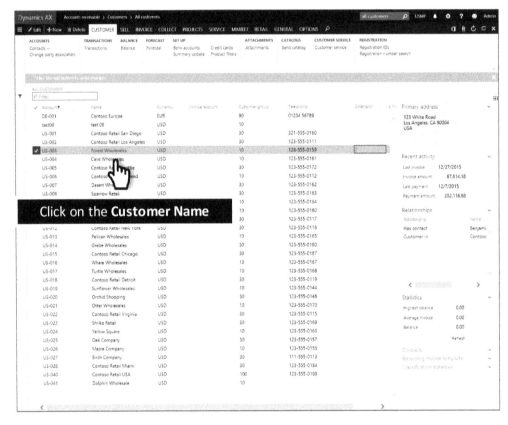

To do this, just click on the customer name or the customer account number.

Accessing detail forms

How to do it...

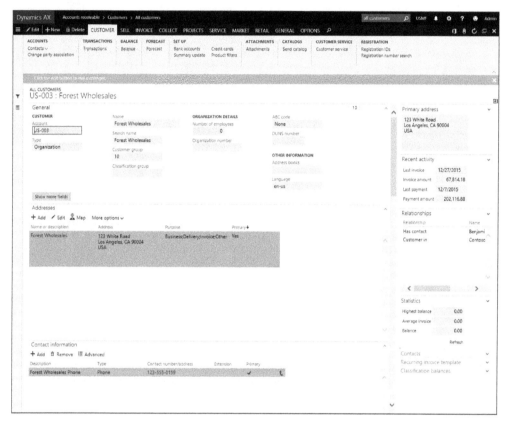

This will open up the detailed view where you can see a lot more of the fields that are related to the record.

da✕c www.dynamicsaxcompanions.com
Dynamics AX Companions
- 83 -
www.blindsquirrelpublishing.com
© 2015 Blind Squirrel Publishing, LLC , All Rights Reserved
BLIND SQUIRREL
PUBLISHING

Accessing the ribbon bar commands

When you are on either the list page view or the details pane you can access additional functions related to the record from the ribbon menu bar at the top of the form.

How to do it...

For example, while on the Customers record you can access all of the functions that are related to the invoicing by clicking on the INVOICE ribbon bar tab.

This will open up the invoice functions and then you can click on the Invoice Journal button.

This will open up the Invoice Journals list page.

Accessing the ribbon bar commands

How to do it…

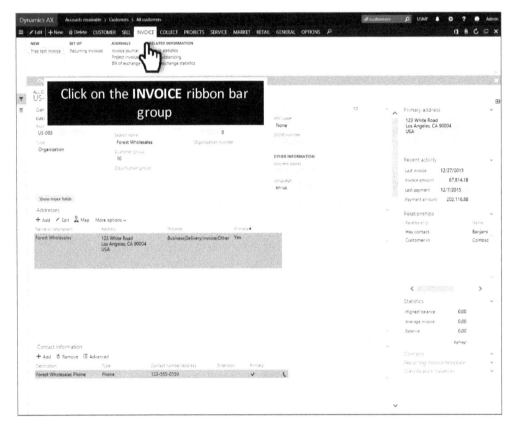

For example, while on the Customers record you can access all of the functions that are related to the invoicing by clicking on the INVOICE ribbon bar tab.

Accessing the ribbon bar commands

How to do it...

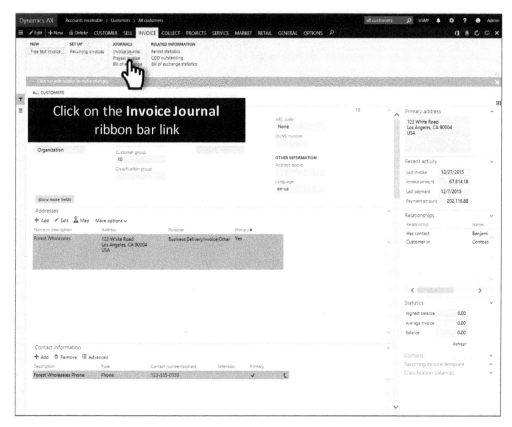

This will open up the invoice functions and then you can click on the Invoice Journal button.

Accessing the ribbon bar commands

How to do it…

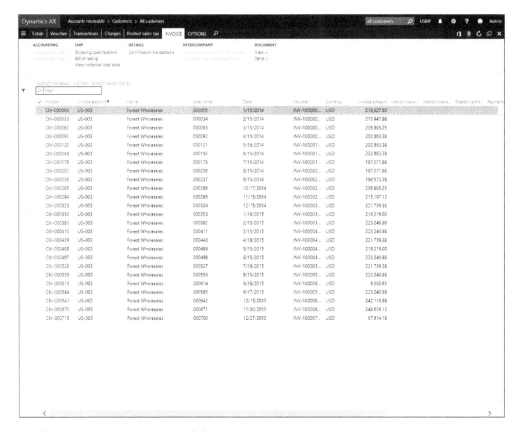

This will open up the Invoice Journals list page.

Collapsing the Ribbon Bar

The ribbon bar, or action bar is a great way to navigate through the functions of the form that you are in. If you are a beginner, then you may want to have this open all of the time so that you can find all of the things that you can do on the form. If you are an expert, or if you don't have a lit of space on your screen then you may want to collapse the bar away and just access it when you need it.

How to do it...

To do this, all you need to do is click on the ^ icon on the bottom right of the ribbon bar.

That will hide the ribbon bar for you so that you have more space on the screen.

You can always access all of the ribbon bar commands just by clicking on the heading. If you want to pin the bar back again, then just click on the Pin on the ribbon bar.

Now the ribbon bar will stay open for you.

 BLIND SQUIRREL PUBLISHING

Collapsing the Ribbon Bar

How to do it…

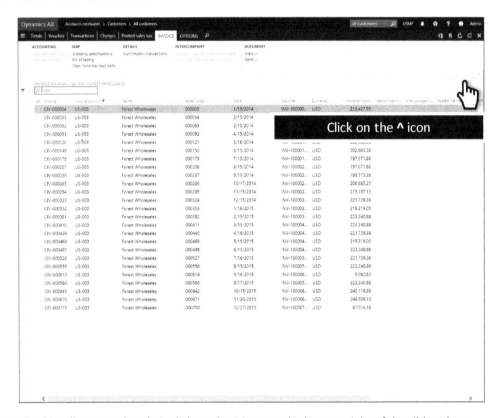

To do this, all you need to do is click on the ^ icon on the bottom right of the ribbon bar.

Collapsing the Ribbon Bar

How to do it...

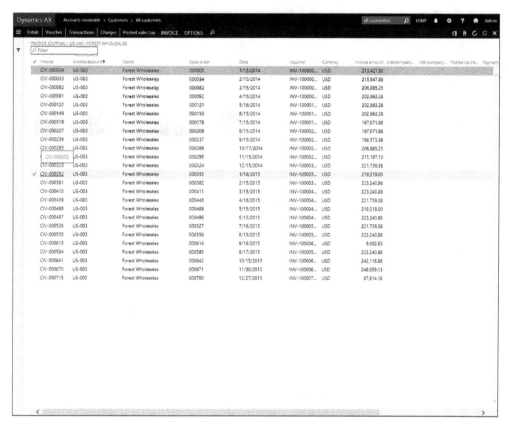

That will hide the ribbon bar for you so that you have more space on the screen.

daxc   www.dynamicsaxcompanions.com
       Dynamics AX Companions

- 91 -

www.blindsquirrelpublishing.com
© 2015 Blind Squirrel Publishing, LLC , All Rights Reserved

BLIND SQUIRREL
PUBLISHING

Collapsing the Ribbon Bar

How to do it…

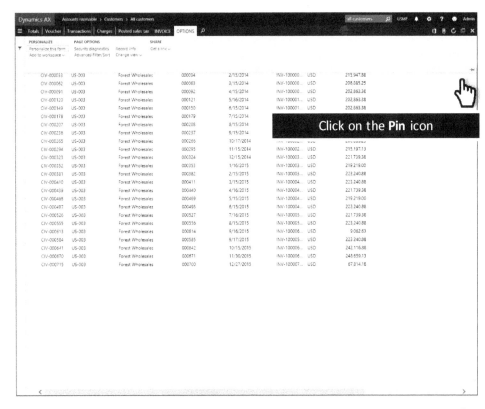

You can always access all of the ribbon bar commands just by clicking on the heading. If you want to pin the bar back again, then just click on the Pin on the ribbon bar.

daxc   www.dynamicsaxcompanions.com
Dynamics AX Companions

- 92 -

www.blindsquirrelpublishing.com
© 2015 Blind Squirrel Publishing, LLC , All Rights Reserved

BLIND SQUIRREL
PUBLISHING

Collapsing the Ribbon Bar

How to do it…

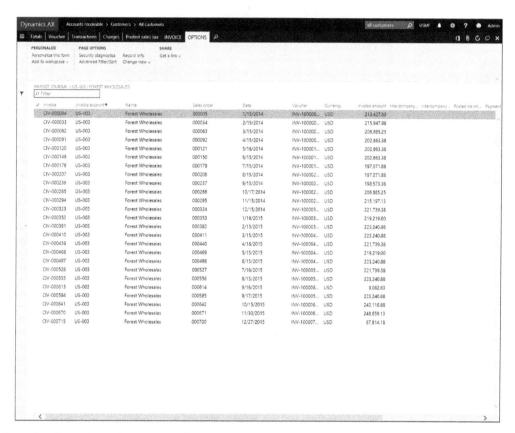

Now the ribbon bar will stay open for you.

Undocking forms

When you open up a new form, in order to manage the screens within the browser, the new Dynamics AX will open up as an overlay form. Sometimes though you may want to see this form, and the form below it. You can do this by undocking the form and it will open up as a new HTML window.

How to do it...

To do this, just click on the Undock icon in the top right hand corner of the form.

This will open up the top window as a new browser window and the original window will change back to the child form.

You can then show the data side by side, or move to other monitors if you have multiple screens.

Even though the window has been opened, this does not mean that the windows are disconnected. If you change the record within the parent form then this will also update the child form.

Undocking forms

How to do it...

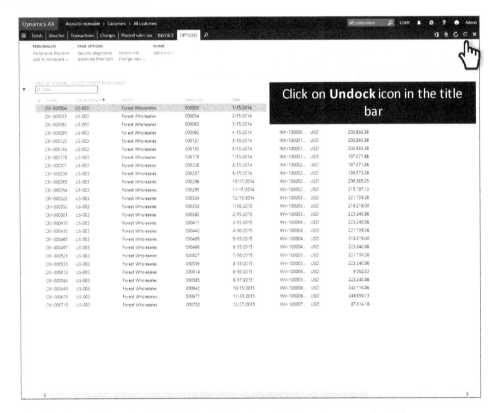

To do this, just click on the Undock icon in the top right hand corner of the form.

daxc   www.dynamicsaxcompanions.com
Dynamics AX Companions

- 96 -

www.blindsquirrelpublishing.com
© 2015 Blind Squirrel Publishing, LLC , All Rights Reserved

BLIND SQUIRREL
PUBLISHING

Undocking forms

How to do it…

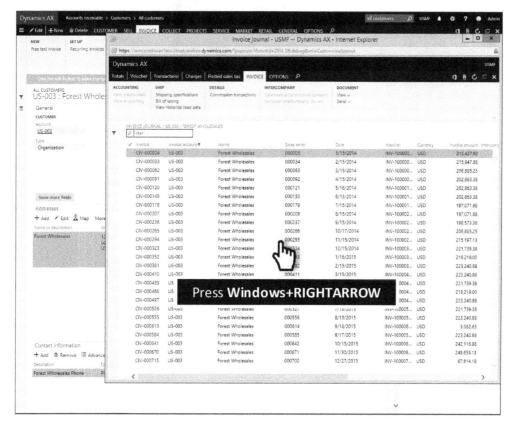

This will open up the top window as a new browser window and the original window will change back to the child form.

daxc
www.dynamicsaxcompanions.com
Dynamics AX Companions
- 97 -
www.blindsquirrelpublishing.com
© 2015 Blind Squirrel Publishing, LLC , All Rights Reserved
BLIND SQUIRREL
PUBLISHING

Undocking forms

How to do it…

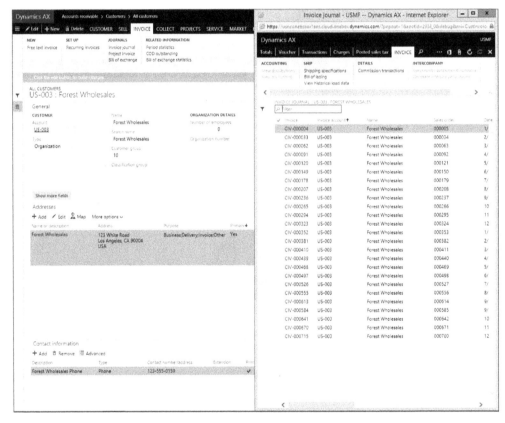

You can then show the data side by side, or move to other monitors if you have multiple screens.

Undocking forms

How to do it…

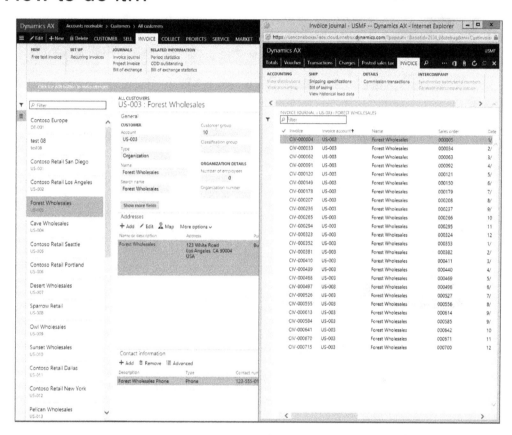

Undocking forms

How to do it...

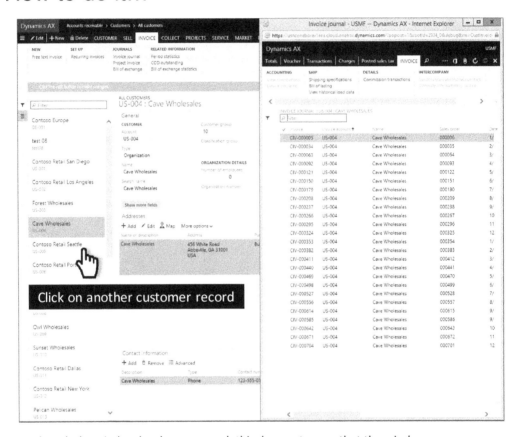

Even though the window has been opened, this does not mean that the windows are disconnected. If you change the record within the parent form then this will also update the child form.

daxc www.dynamicsaxcompanions.com
Dynamics AX Companions

- 100 -

www.blindsquirrelpublishing.com
© 2015 Blind Squirrel Publishing, LLC , All Rights Reserved

 BLIND SQUIRREL PUBLISHING

Using the list filter

When you are in the detail view within the forms, you don't need to return back to the list page each time to navigate from record to record. You can show the list filter feature to navigate through all of the records.

How to do it...

To view the list filter, just click on the List icon on the left hand side of the form.

This will open up a panel on the left hand side that shows you a quick view to all of the records that you can switch to.

If you want to search for records using the filter list then all you need to do is type in part of the name that you want to search on

This will filter the data out to any record that matches your search and also change the detail panel to show the first record that matches.

Using the list filter

How to do it...

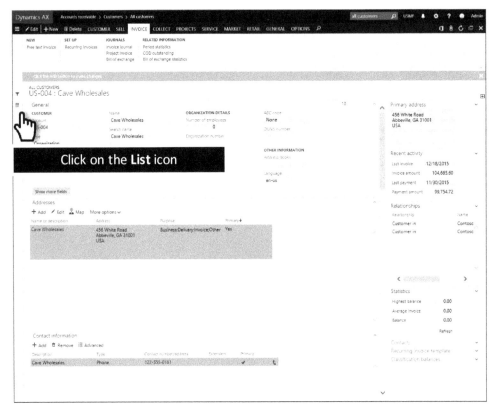

To view the list filter, just click on the List icon on the left hand side of the form.

daxc   www.dynamicsaxcompanions.com
        Dynamics AX Companions

- 102 -

www.blindsquirrelpublishing.com
© 2015 Blind Squirrel Publishing, LLC , All Rights Reserved

BLIND SQUIRREL
PUBLISHING

Using the list filter

How to do it…

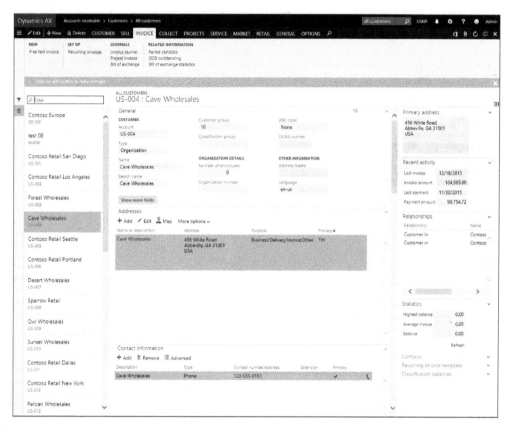

This will open up a panel on the left hand side that shows you a quick view to all of the records that you can switch to.

daxc   www.dynamicsaxcompanions.com
       Dynamics AX Companions

- 103 -

www.blindsquirrelpublishing.com
© 2015 Blind Squirrel Publishing, LLC , All Rights Reserved

BLIND SQUIRREL
PUBLISHING

Using the list filter

How to do it…

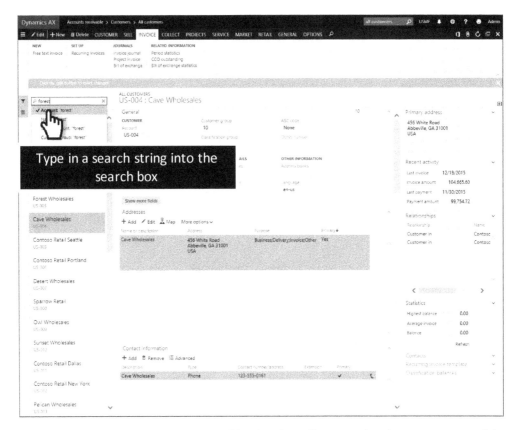

If you want to search for records using the filter list then all you need to do is type in part of the name that you want to search on

Using the list filter

How to do it…

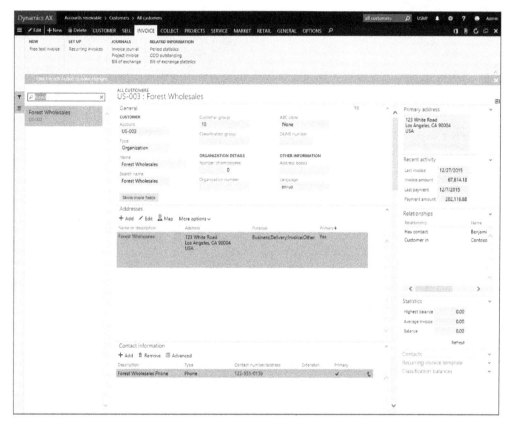

This will filter the data out to any record that matches your search and also change the detail panel to show the first record that matches.

Zooming

Because the new Dynamics AX is a HTML client then you can also take advantage of some of the features of HTML5 which includes the responsive web design. What this means is that if you zoom in and out the forms will adjust themselves to match the page real estate.

How to do it...

If you zoom out then you will see that the form fields will re-layout to take advantage of the extra space that is available.

If you zoom in, then the fields will re-arrange themselves so that they are not falling off the right of the page and layout into a longer form.

You can return back to the default zoom setting by pressing CTRL+0.

 www.dynamicsaxcompanions.com
Dynamics AX Companions

- 107 -

www.blindsquirrelpublishing.com
© 2015 Blind Squirrel Publishing, LLC , All Rights Reserved

 BLIND SQUIRREL
PUBLISHING

Zooming

How to do it…

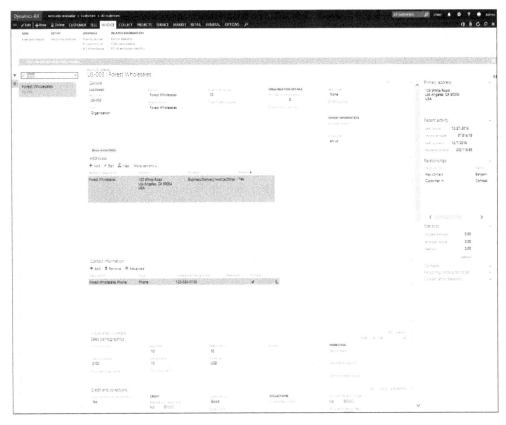

If you zoom out then you will see that the form fields will re-layout to take advantage of the extra space that is available.

daxc www.dynamicsaxcompanions.com
Dynamics AX Companions

- 108 -

www.blindsquirrelpublishing.com
© 2015 Blind Squirrel Publishing, LLC , All Rights Reserved

BLIND SQUIRREL
PUBLISHING

Zooming

How to do it…

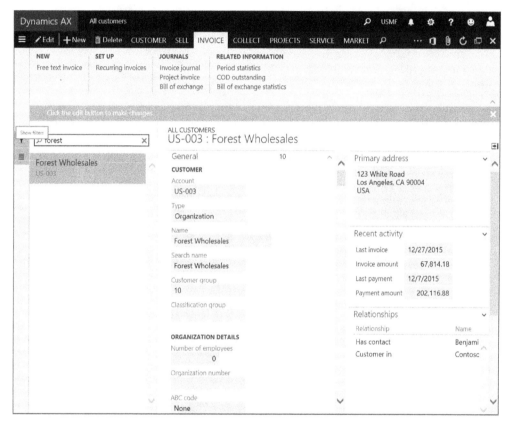

If you zoom in, then the fields will re-arrange themselves so that they are not falling off the right of the page and layout into a longer form.

Zooming

How to do it...

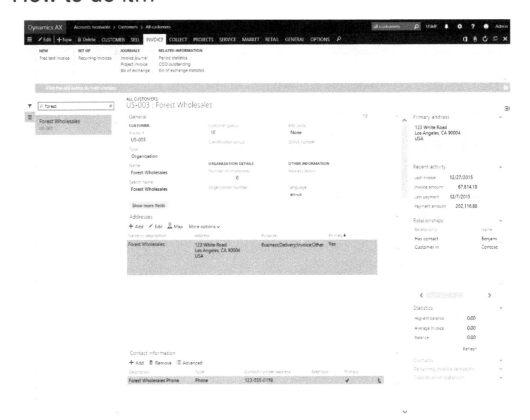

You can return back to the default zoom setting by pressing CTRL+0.

www.dynamicsaxcompanions.com
Dynamics AX Companions

- 110 -

www.blindsquirrelpublishing.com
© 2015 Blind Squirrel Publishing, LLC , All Rights Reserved

BLIND SQUIRREL
PUBLISHING

PERSONALIZATION

Not everyone is happy with all of the data that is available on the default forms within Dynamics AX, and that's expected. Some people want to see less information, others may want to see more. Luckily you can do this directly from the Dynamics AX client and you don't have to customize the system at all.

Hiding fields

The first type or personalization that you may want to do is to hide some of the extra fields that you are not interested in.

How to do it...

For example, if you are on the customers list page, you may not want to see the Extension field. To hide the field, start off by right-mouse-clicking on the field heading.

Then click on the Personalize Extension menu option.

This will open up the Personalization options for the field.

To hide the field, just check the Hide option for the field

Now the field is hidden.

Hiding fields

How to do it…

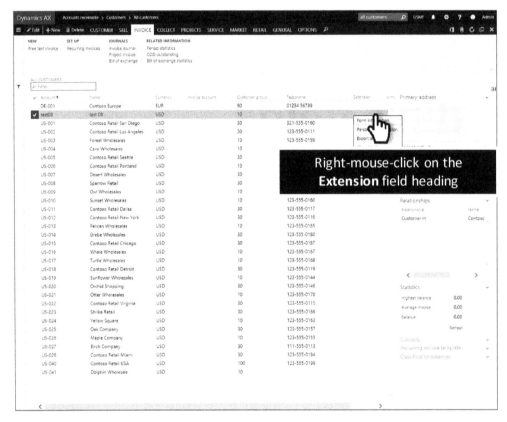

For example, if you are on the customers list page, you may not want to see the Extension field. To hide the field, start off by right-mouse-clicking on the field heading.

Hiding fields

How to do it...

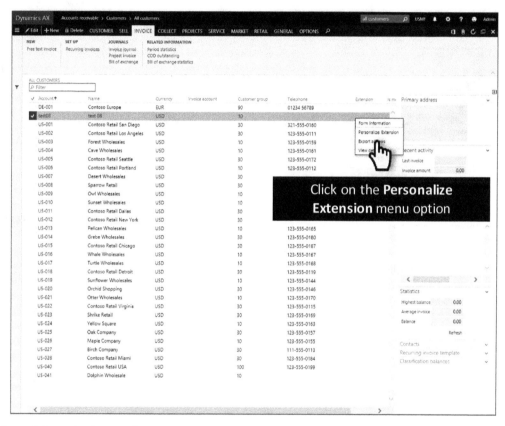

Then click on the Personalize Extension menu option.

daxc www.dynamicsaxcompanions.com
Dynamics AX Companions

- 115 -

www.blindsquirrelpublishing.com
© 2015 Blind Squirrel Publishing, LLC , All Rights Reserved

BLIND SQUIRREL
PUBLISHING

Hiding fields

How to do it...

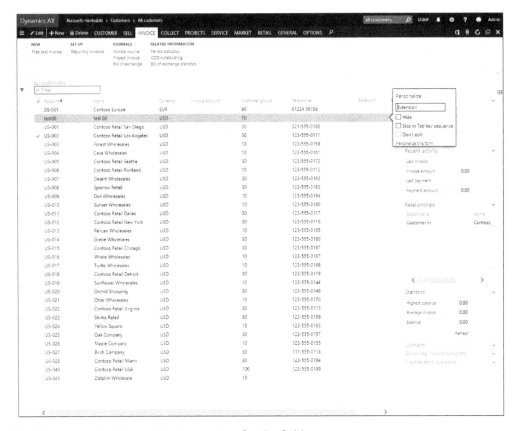

This will open up the Personalization options for the field.

daxc   www.dynamicsaxcompanions.com
Dynamics AX Companions

- 116 -

www.blindsquirrelpublishing.com
© 2015 Blind Squirrel Publishing, LLC , All Rights Reserved

BLIND SQUIRREL
PUBLISHING

Hiding fields

How to do it...

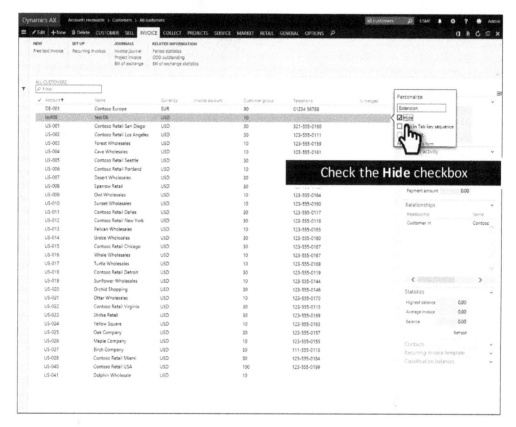

To hide the field, just check the Hide option for the field

Hiding fields

How to do it…

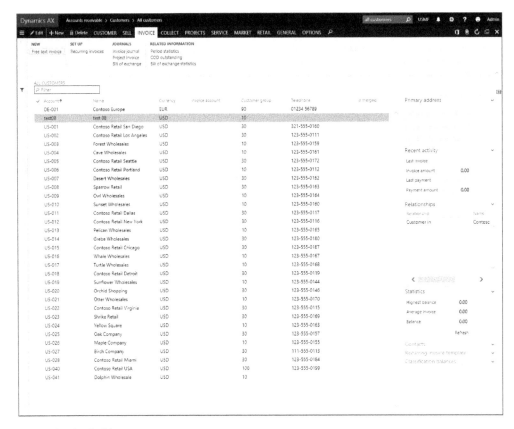

Now the field is hidden.

Unhiding fields

If you have hidden a field, it is not gone forever. You can easily re-enable it so that you can reuse them again.

How to do it...

In order to re-enable the hidden fields you need to turn on the option that will allow you to see all of the hidden fields so that you can manipulate the personalization. To do this, click on the OPTIONS ribbon bar button.

Then click on the Personalize this form menu item within the Action panel.

This will open up the Personalization toolbar.

Now click on the Show/Hide icon in the personalization bar to

When the Options ribbon bar is shown click on the Show hidden fields/columns link within the Personalize button group.

When the Options ribbon bar is shown click on the Show hidden fields/columns link within the Personalize button group.

This will allow you to see the hidden fields.

 www.dynamicsaxcompanions.com
Dynamics AX Companions

- 119 -

www.blindsquirrelpublishing.com
© 2015 Blind Squirrel Publishing, LLC , All Rights Reserved

 BLIND SQUIRREL
PUBLISHING

Unhiding fields

How to do it…

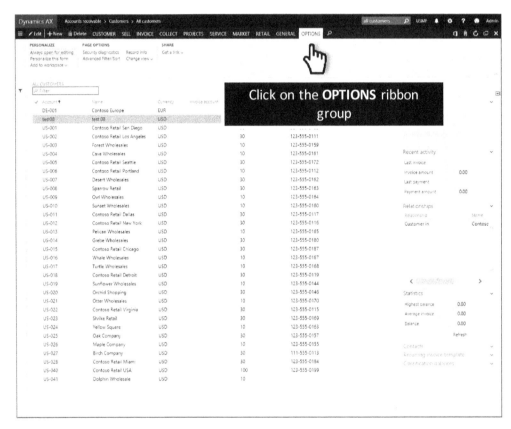

In order to re-enable the hidden fields you need to turn on the option that will allow you to see all of the hidden fields so that you can manipulate the personalization. To do this, click on the OPTIONS ribbon bar button.

Unhiding fields

How to do it...

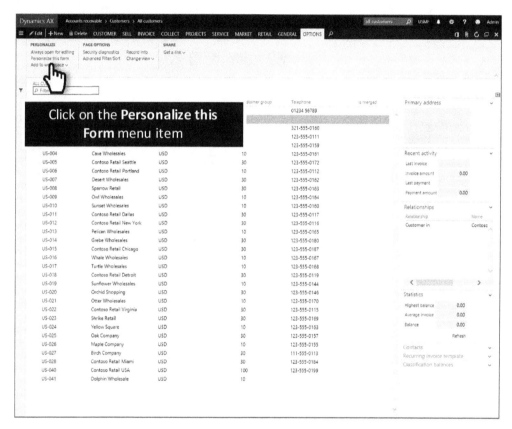

Then click on the Personalize this form menu item within the Action panel.

daxc www.dynamicsaxcompanions.com
Dynamics AX Companions
- 121 -
www.blindsquirrelpublishing.com
© 2015 Blind Squirrel Publishing, LLC , All Rights Reserved
BLIND SQUIRREL PUBLISHING

Unhiding fields

How to do it…

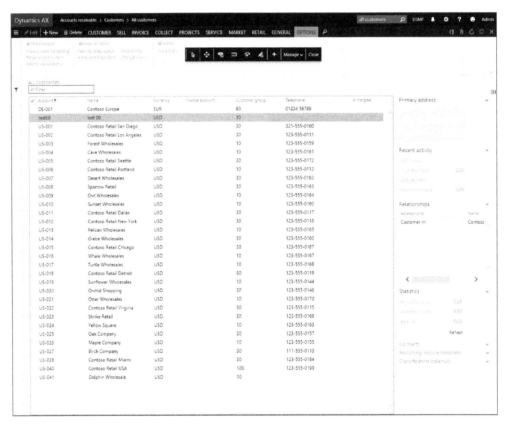

This will open up the Personalization toolbar.

dax   www.dynamicsaxcompanions.com
Dynamics AX Companions
www.blindsquirrelpublishing.com
© 2015 Blind Squirrel Publishing, LLC , All Rights Reserved
BLIND SQUIRREL PUBLISHING

Unhiding fields

How to do it…

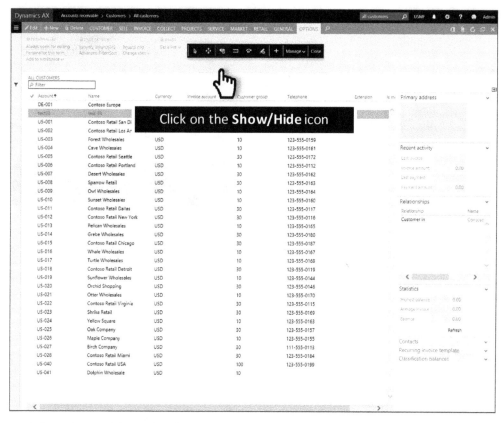

Now click on the Show/Hide icon in the personalization bar to

Unhiding fields

How to do it…

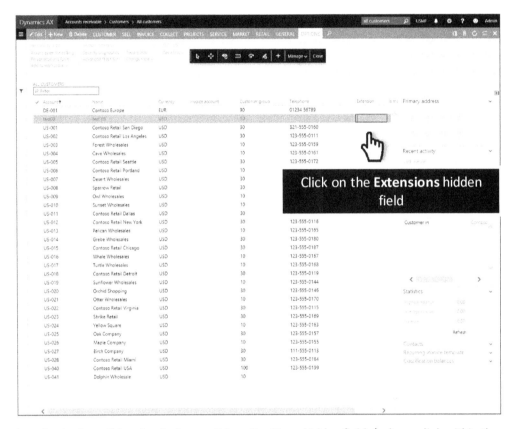

When the Options ribbon bar is shown click on the Show hidden fields/columns link within the Personalize button group.

Unhiding fields

How to do it...

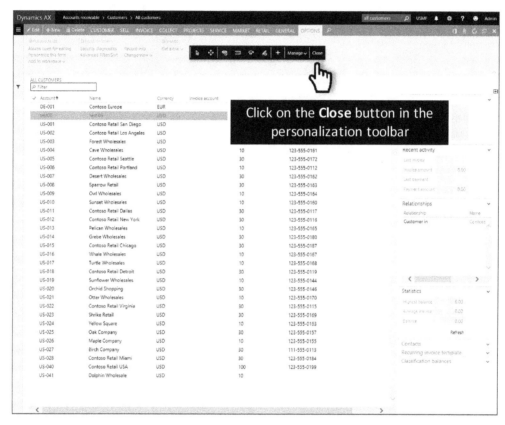

Click on the **Close** button in the personalization toolbar

When the Options ribbon bar is shown click on the Show hidden fields/columns link within the Personalize button group.

 www.dynamicsaxcompanions.com
Dynamics AX Companions
- 125 -
www.blindsquirrelpublishing.com
© 2015 Blind Squirrel Publishing, LLC , All Rights Reserved
BLIND SQUIRREL PUBLISHING

Unhiding fields

How to do it…

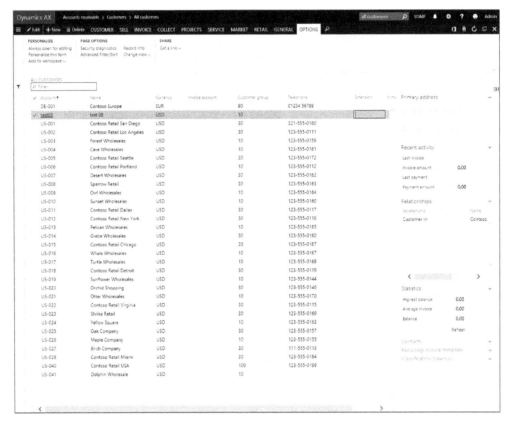

This will allow you to see the hidden fields.

dažc   www.dynamicsaxcompanions.com
Dynamics AX Companions

www.blindsquirrelpublishing.com
© 2015 Blind Squirrel Publishing, LLC , All Rights Reserved

 BLIND SQUIRREL
PUBLISHING

Adding additional fields

Another personalization that you can perform is the adding of additional fields to the forms that may not already be on the form.

How to do it...

To do this, start off by clicking on the Options Action Panel.

Then click on the Personalize this Form action menu item.

This will open up a personalization toolbar, and you just need to click on the + icon to switch to the add mode.

Now just click on the data grid that you want to add the field to.

This will then open up a Add a Field dialog and all you need to do is check the additional fields that you want to show on the form.

After you have selected the fields, click on the Insert button.

To finish the personalization, just click on the Close button within the Personalization tool bar.

When you return back to the form you will see that the fields have been added to the list page.

Adding additional fields

How to do it...

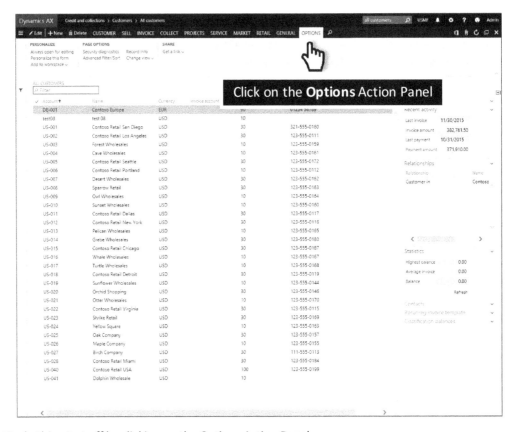

To do this, start off by clicking on the Options Action Panel.

daxc   www.dynamicsaxcompanions.com
Dynamics AX Companions
- 128 -
www.blindsquirrelpublishing.com
© 2015 Blind Squirrel Publishing, LLC , All Rights Reserved

BLIND SQUIRREL
PUBLISHING

Adding additional fields

How to do it…

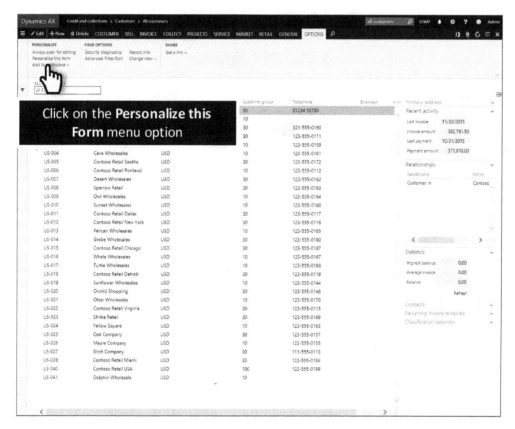

Then click on the Personalize this Form action menu item.

daxc
www.dynamicsaxcompanions.com
Dynamics AX Companions

- 129 -

www.blindsquirrelpublishing.com
© 2015 Blind Squirrel Publishing, LLC , All Rights Reserved

BLIND SQUIRREL
PUBLISHING

Adding additional fields

How to do it…

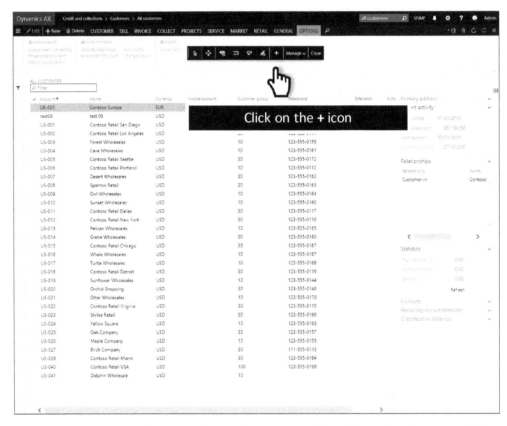

This will open up a personalization toolbar, and you just need to click on the + icon to switch to the add mode.

da✗c www.dynamicsaxcompanions.com
Dynamics AX Companions

Adding additional fields

How to do it...

Now just click on the data grid that you want to add the field to.

Adding additional fields

How to do it…

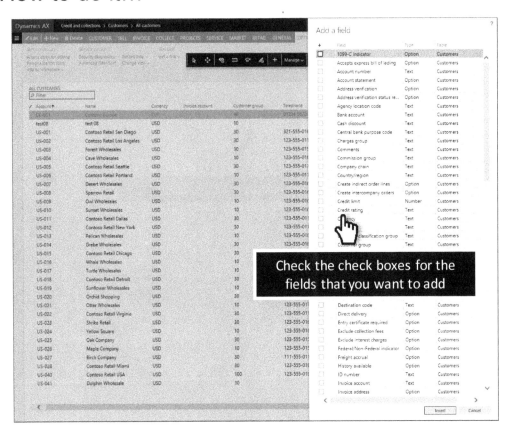

This will then open up a Add a Field dialog and all you need to do is check the additional fields that you want to show on the form.

Adding additional fields

How to do it…

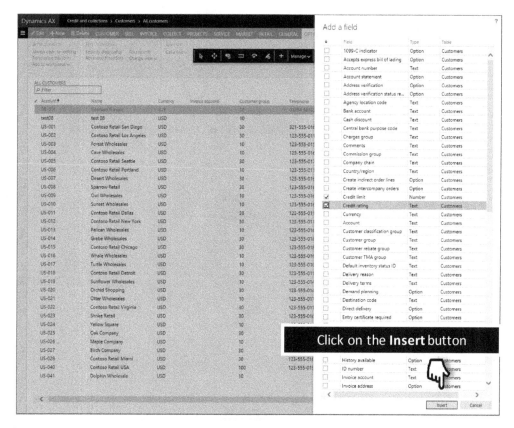

After you have selected the fields, click on the Insert button.

Adding additional fields

How to do it...

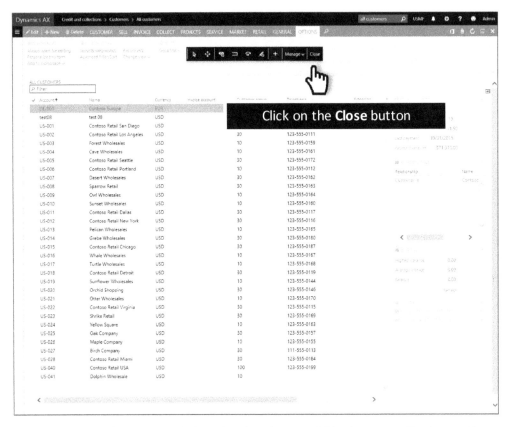

To finish the personalization, just click on the Close button within the Personalization tool bar.

www.dynamicsaxcompanions.com
Dynamics AX Companions

- 134 -

www.blindsquirrelpublishing.com
© 2015 Blind Squirrel Publishing, LLC , All Rights Reserved

BLIND SQUIRREL
PUBLISHING

Adding additional fields

How to do it...

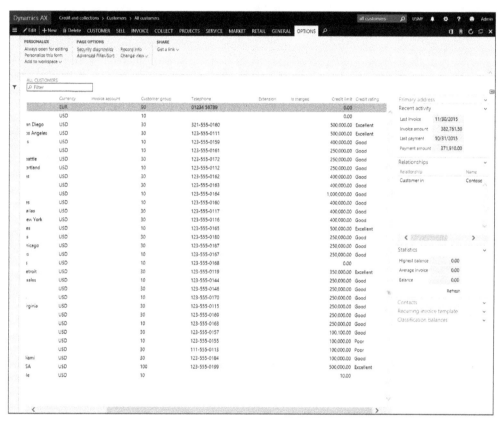

When you return back to the form you will see that the fields have been added to the list page.

www.dynamicsaxcompanions.com
Dynamics AX Companions

- 135 -

www.blindsquirrelpublishing.com
© 2015 Blind Squirrel Publishing, LLC , All Rights Reserved

BLIND SQUIRREL
PUBLISHING

Moving fields

Some fields may be more important to you than others, and sometimes you may want to move the fields around and show them in different orders.

How to do it...

To move a field, start off by clicking on the Options Action Panel.

Then click on the Personalize this Form action menu item.

Then when personalization toolbar is shown, click on the move button (the one that looks like a compass).

This will then change the form into move mode. All you need to do is select the field that you want to move and drag it to its new position.

To finish the personalization, just click on the Close button within the Personalization tool bar.

When you return to the form you will see that the fields have been moved for you.

Moving fields

How to do it…

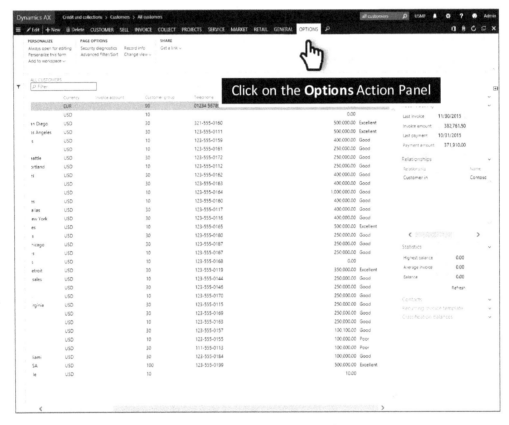

To move a field, start off by clicking on the Options Action Panel.

www.dynamicsaxcompanions.com
Dynamics AX Companions

- 138 -

www.blindsquirrelpublishing.com
© 2015 Blind Squirrel Publishing, LLC , All Rights Reserved

BLIND SQUIRREL
PUBLISHING

Moving fields

How to do it…

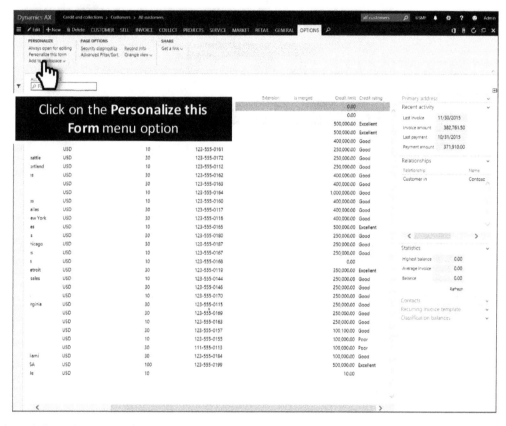

Then click on the Personalize this Form action menu item.

daxc www.dynamicsaxcompanions.com
Dynamics AX Companions

- 139 -

www.blindsquirrelpublishing.com
© 2015 Blind Squirrel Publishing, LLC , All Rights Reserved

BLIND SQUIRREL
PUBLISHING

Moving fields

How to do it…

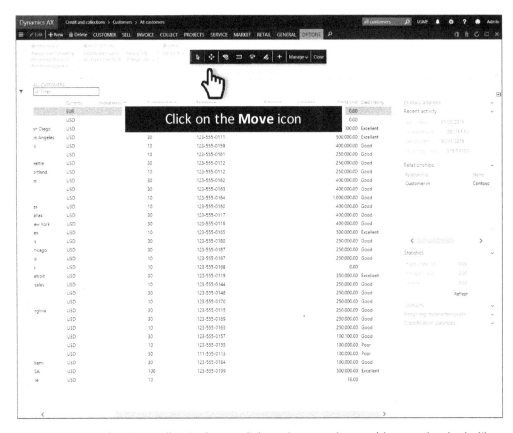

Then when personalization toolbar is shown, click on the move button (the one that looks like a compass).

www.dynamicsaxcompanions.com
Dynamics AX Companions

- 140 -

www.blindsquirrelpublishing.com
© 2015 Blind Squirrel Publishing, LLC , All Rights Reserved

BLIND SQUIRREL
PUBLISHING

Moving fields

How to do it...

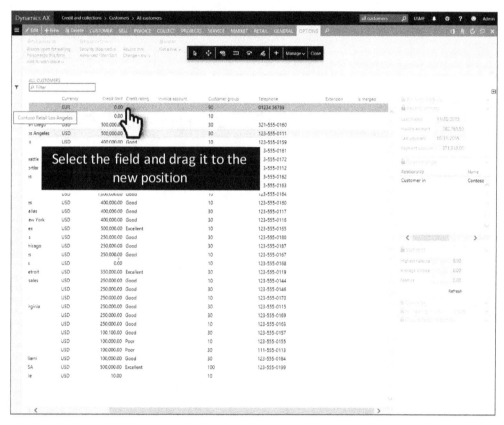

This will then change the form into move mode. All you need to do is select the field that you want to move and drag it to its new position.

Moving fields

How to do it...

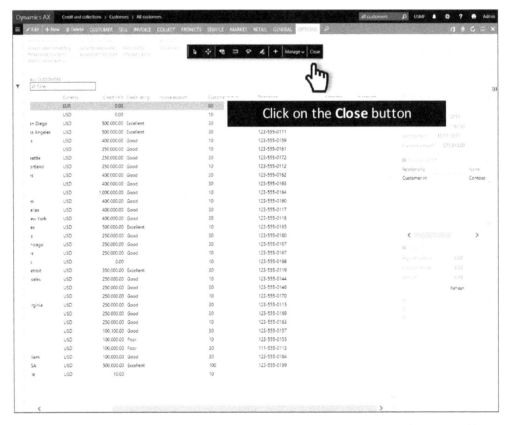

To finish the personalization, just click on the Close button within the Personalization tool bar.

www.dynamicsaxcompanions.com
Dynamics AX Companions

- 142 -

www.blindsquirrelpublishing.com
© 2015 Blind Squirrel Publishing, LLC , All Rights Reserved

BLIND SQUIRREL
PUBLISHING

Moving fields

How to do it...

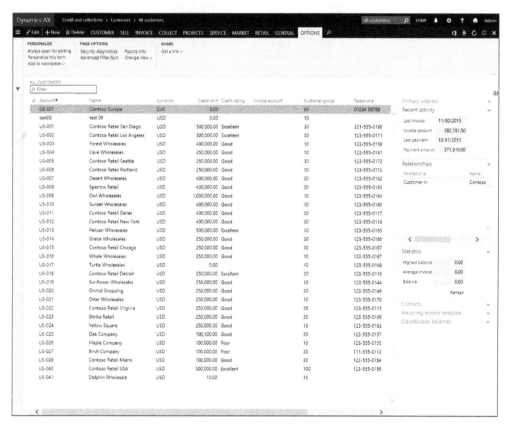

When you return to the form you will see that the fields have been moved for you.

Filtering lists

The list pages are a great way for you to create simple reports directly from the application, but you probably don't want to see all of the data. We have shown you how you can filter based off the main data, but you can also filter based on any of the fields that are shown on the form.

How to do it...

To filter any of the fields, just click on the Down Arrow icon at the right end of the field heading to pull up the field options.

If you click on the filter criteria you will see that there are a number of different ways that you can filter including contains, begins with, etc.

Then type in the filter that you want to apply to the field.

And then click on the Apply button to apply the filter.

When you return back to the form you will see that the list page has been filtered to just show you the information that matches.

www.blindsquirrelpublishing.com
© 2015 Blind Squirrel Publishing, LLC , All Rights Reserved

BLIND SQUIRREL
PUBLISHING

Filtering lists

How to do it...

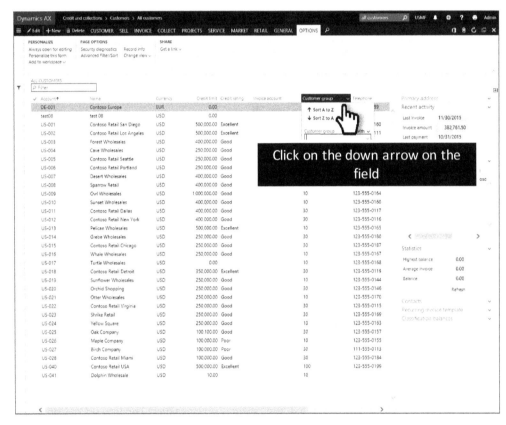

To filter any of the fields, just click on the Down Arrow icon at the right end of the field heading to pull up the field options.

Filtering lists

How to do it…

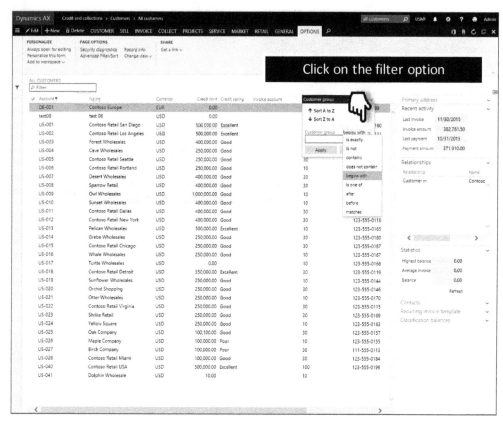

If you click on the filter criteria you will see that there are a number of different ways that you can filter including contains, begins with, etc.

Filtering lists

How to do it…

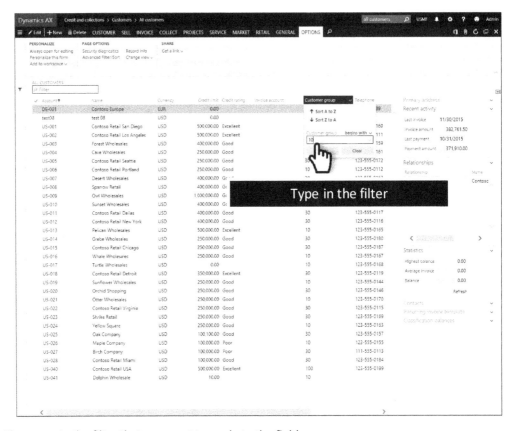

Then type in the filter that you want to apply to the field.

da✕c   www.dynamicsaxcompanions.com
       Dynamics AX Companions

- 148 -

www.blindsquirrelpublishing.com
© 2015 Blind Squirrel Publishing, LLC , All Rights Reserved

BLIND SQUIRREL
PUBLISHING

Filtering lists

How to do it…

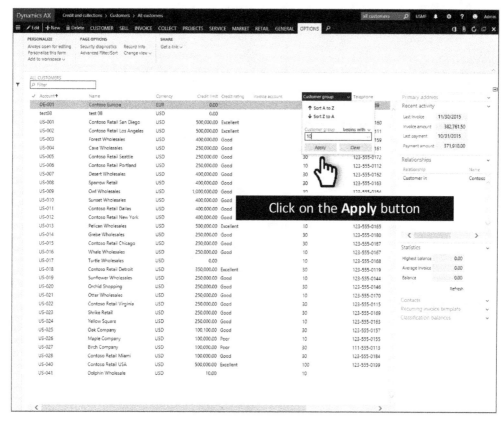

And then click on the Apply button to apply the filter.

daxc   www.dynamicsaxcompanions.com
Dynamics AX Companions

Filtering lists

How to do it…

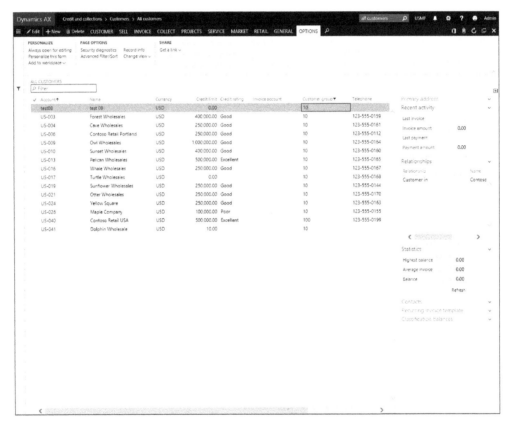

When you return back to the form you will see that the list page has been filtered to just show you the information that matches.

www.blindsquirrelpublishing.com
© 2015 Blind Squirrel Publishing, LLC , All Rights Reserved

BLIND SQUIRREL
PUBLISHING

Saving user personalization

After you have tweaked all of the forms and made them look just like you want and with just the fields that you want, you may want to save the configuration away just in case you want to share them with other users or if you need to reconfigure the form some time in the future.

How to do it...

To do this, all you need to do is click on the OPTIONS ribbon bar link.

Then click on the Personalize this Form menu item.

Then the personalization toolbar is displayed, click on the Manage button.

And then click on the Export menu item.

This will create an XML configuration file with all of the personalization's that you made. All you need to do is click on the Save button.

When the Save As dialog box is displayed, just navigate to where you want to file the personalization file away to and then click on the Save button.

When you are done just click on the Close button within the Personalization tool bar.

 www.dynamicsaxcompanions.com
Dynamics AX Companions

- 151 -

www.blindsquirrelpublishing.com
© 2015 Blind Squirrel Publishing, LLC , All Rights Reserved

 BLIND SQUIRREL
PUBLISHING

Saving user personalization

How to do it...

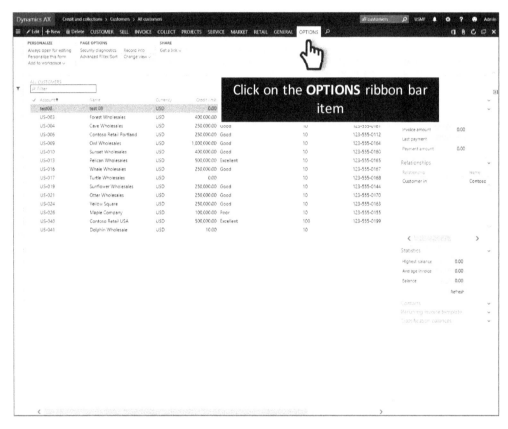

To do this, all you need to do is click on the OPTIONS ribbon bar link.

Saving user personalization

How to do it...

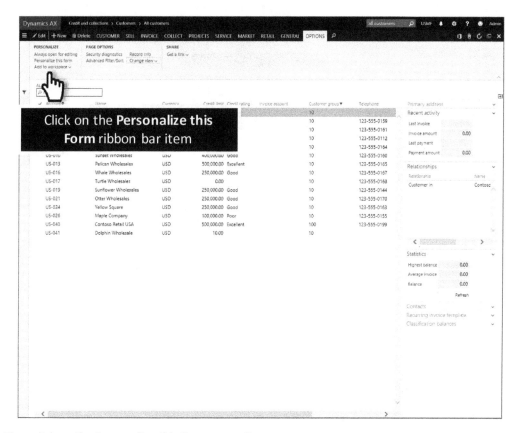

Then click on the Personalize this Form menu item.

Saving user personalization

How to do it…

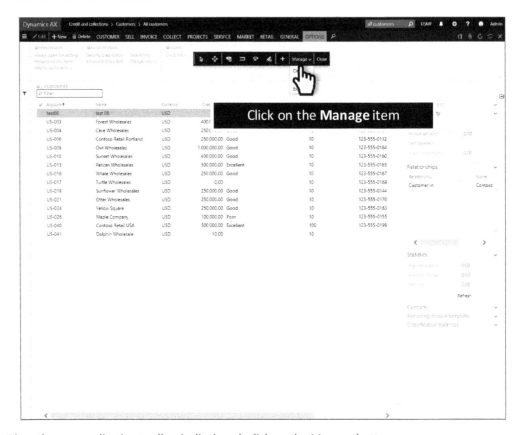

Then the personalization toolbar is displayed, click on the Manage button.

daxc   www.dynamicsaxcompanions.com
Dynamics AX Companions
- 154 -
www.blindsquirrelpublishing.com
© 2015 Blind Squirrel Publishing, LLC , All Rights Reserved
BLIND SQUIRREL PUBLISHING

Saving user personalization

How to do it…

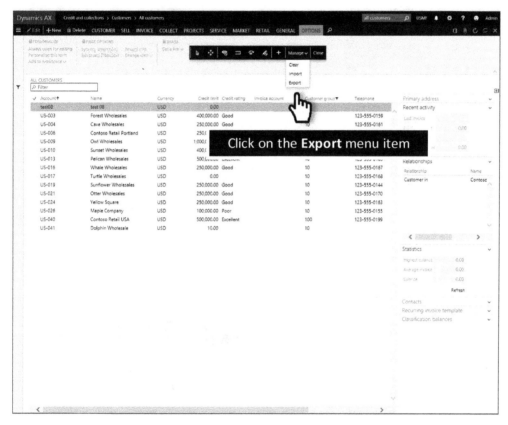

And then click on the Export menu item.

daXc www.dynamicsaxcompanions.com
Dynamics AX Companions

- 155 -

www.blindsquirrelpublishing.com
© 2015 Blind Squirrel Publishing, LLC , All Rights Reserved

BLIND SQUIRREL
PUBLISHING

Saving user personalization

How to do it…

This will create an XML configuration file with all of the personalization's that you made. All you need to do is click on the Save button.

daxc   www.dynamicsaxcompanions.com
Dynamics AX Companions

- 156 -

www.blindsquirrelpublishing.com
© 2015 Blind Squirrel Publishing, LLC , All Rights Reserved

BLIND SQUIRREL
PUBLISHING

Saving user personalization

How to do it…

When the Save As dialog box is displayed, just navigate to where you want to file the personalization file away to and then click on the Save button.

daxc   www.dynamicsaxcompanions.com
       Dynamics AX Companions

- 157 -

www.blindsquirrelpublishing.com
© 2015 Blind Squirrel Publishing, LLC , All Rights Reserved

BLIND SQUIRREL PUBLISHING

Saving user personalization

How to do it...

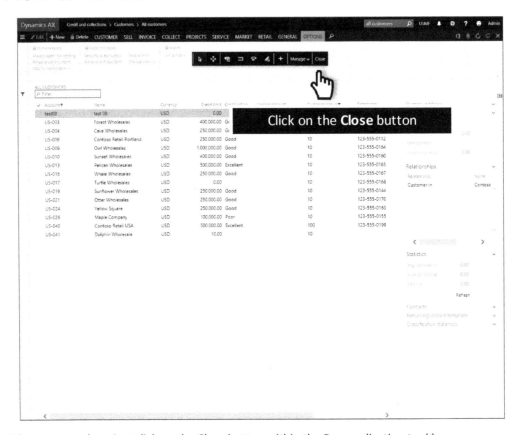

When you are done just click on the Close button within the Personalization tool bar.

Importing custom views into other users

Once you have created an export of the user personalization then you can share it with other users and then they can also apply it to their forms which makes it a great way to quickly personalize the system.

How to do it...

To do this, all you need to do is click on the OPTIONS ribbon bar.

Then click on the Personalize this Form menu item.

Then the personalization toolbar is displayed, click on the Manage button.

And then click on the Import menu item.

This will open up the Select a file dialog box and you can then click on the Browse button.

This will open up a file explorer. Just navigate to the location where the personalization's are stored and then click on the Open button.

This will apply the change and return you back to the form. You will notice though that no changes have been made yet – all you need to do is refresh the page – so press F5.

This will update the form and now you will see the new configuration of the form based on the personalization file that you just imported.

daxc www.dynamicsaxcompanions.com
Dynamics AX Companions

- 159 -

www.blindsquirrelpublishing.com
© 2015 Blind Squirrel Publishing, LLC , All Rights Reserved

 BLIND SQUIRREL PUBLISHING

Importing custom views into other users

How to do it…

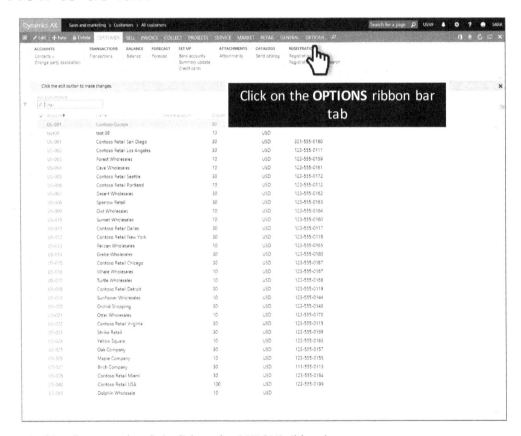

To do this, all you need to do is click on the OPTIONS ribbon bar.

Importing custom views into other users

How to do it…

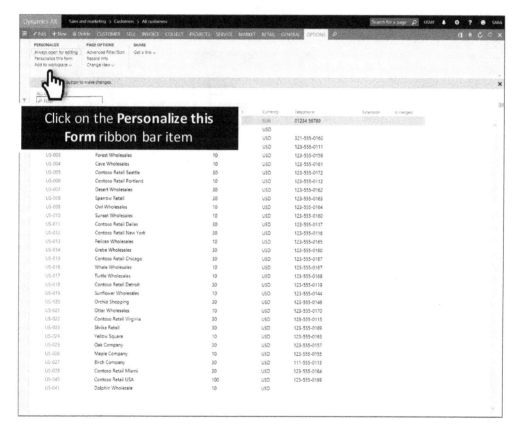

Then click on the Personalize this Form menu item.

daxc   www.dynamicsaxcompanions.com
Dynamics AX Companions

- 161 -

www.blindsquirrelpublishing.com
© 2015 Blind Squirrel Publishing, LLC , All Rights Reserved

BLIND SQUIRREL
PUBLISHING

Importing custom views into other users

How to do it…

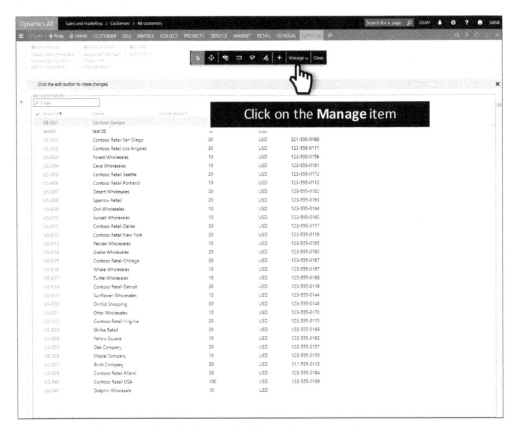

Then the personalization toolbar is displayed, click on the Manage button.

Importing custom views into other users

How to do it…

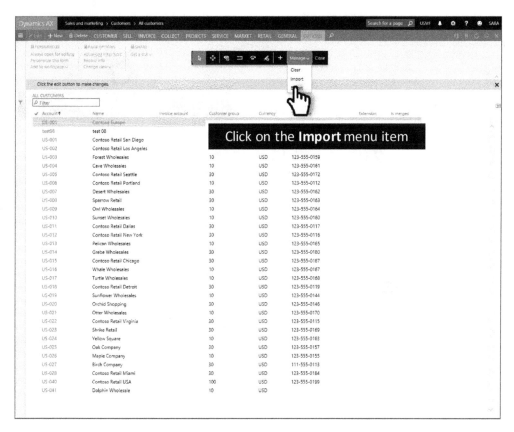

And then click on the Import menu item.

daxc   www.dynamicsaxcompanions.com
Dynamics AX Companions

BLIND SQUIRREL
PUBLISHING

Importing custom views into other users

How to do it…

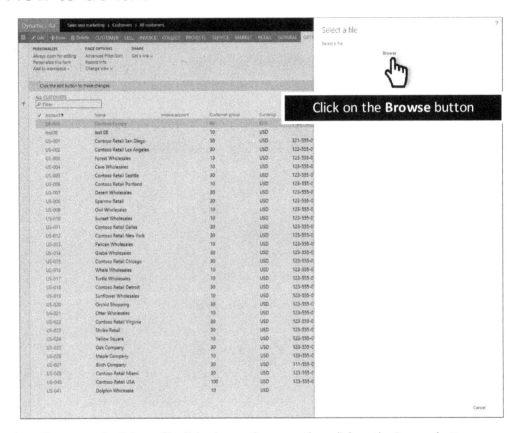

This will open up the Select a file dialog box and you can then click on the Browse button.

Importing custom views into other users

How to do it…

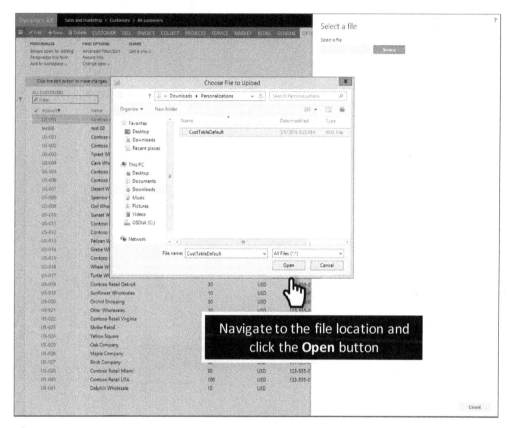

Navigate to the file location and click the **Open** button

This will open up a file explorer. Just navigate to the location where the personalization's are stored and then click on the Open button.

Importing custom views into other users

How to do it…

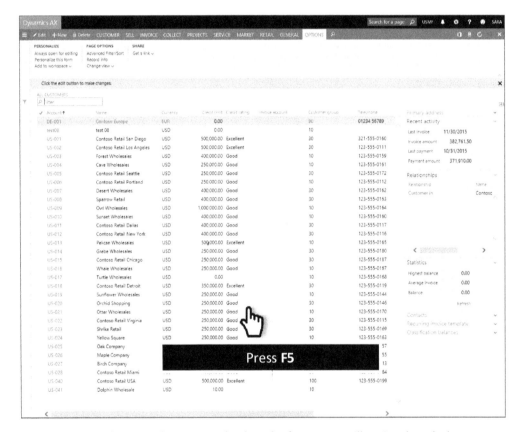

This will apply the change and return you back to the form. You will notice though that no changes have been made yet – all you need to do is refresh the page – so press F5.

This will update the form and now you will see the new configuration of the form based on the personalization file that you just imported.

daxc   www.dynamicsaxcompanions.com
Dynamics AX Companions

- 166 -

www.blindsquirrelpublishing.com
© 2015 Blind Squirrel Publishing, LLC , All Rights Reserved

BLIND SQUIRREL
PUBLISHING

Using filter panel

Another way that you can filter and search for data is through the Filter Panel which is hidden on the left hand side of the form.

How to do it...

To access the filter panel just click on the Filter icon on the left hand side of the page.

This will open up the filter panel and you will see all of the current fields that you can filter on.

To filter the list page, just type in the filter string into the field box.

And then click on the Apply button. You will then see that the list page has been filtered to just the records that match the filter.

To return back to the original state, all you need to do is click on the Reset button and the filters will be removed.

www.dynamicsaxcompanions.com
Dynamics AX Companions

- 167 -

www.blindsquirrelpublishing.com
© 2015 Blind Squirrel Publishing, LLC , All Rights Reserved

BLIND SQUIRREL
PUBLISHING

Using filter panel

How to do it…

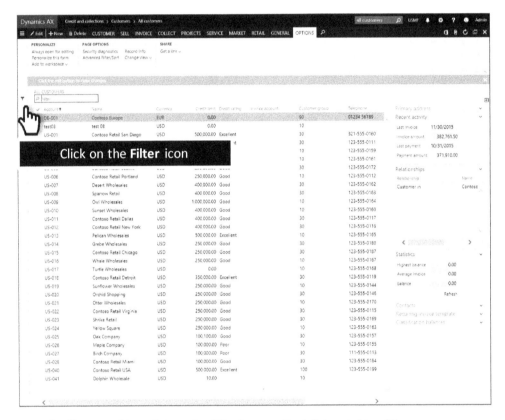

To access the filter panel just click on the Filter icon on the left hand side of the page.

Using filter panel

How to do it...

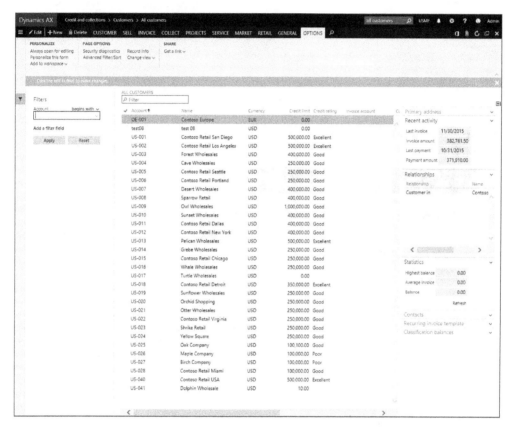

This will open up the filter panel and you will see all of the current fields that you can filter on.

daxc   www.dynamicsaxcompanions.com
       Dynamics AX Companions
       - 169 -
       www.blindsquirrelpublishing.com
       © 2015 Blind Squirrel Publishing, LLC , All Rights Reserved
       BLIND SQUIRREL
       PUBLISHING

Using filter panel

How to do it…

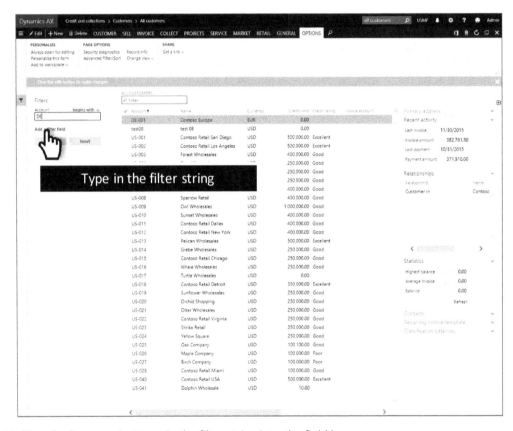

To filter the list page, just type in the filter string into the field box.

daxc www.dynamicsaxcompanions.com
Dynamics AX Companions

- 170 -

www.blindsquirrelpublishing.com
© 2015 Blind Squirrel Publishing, LLC , All Rights Reserved

BLIND SQUIRREL
PUBLISHING

Using filter panel

How to do it...

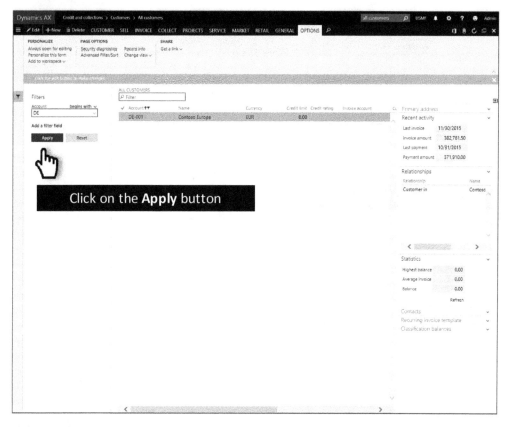

And then click on the Apply button. You will then see that the list page has been filtered to just the records that match the filter.

Using filter panel

How to do it…

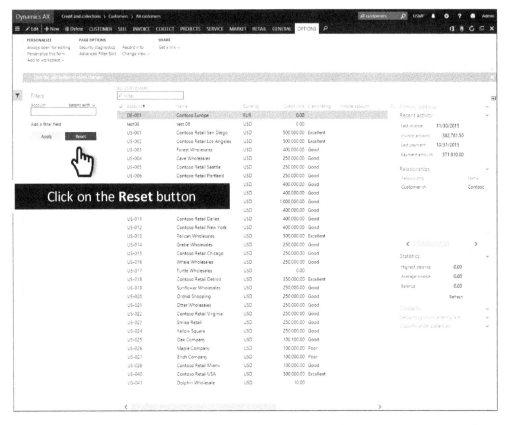

To return back to the original state, all you need to do is click on the Reset button and the filters will be removed.

daxc   www.dynamicsaxcompanions.com
Dynamics AX Companions
- 172 -
www.blindsquirrelpublishing.com
© 2015 Blind Squirrel Publishing, LLC , All Rights Reserved
BLIND SQUIRREL
PUBLISHING

Adding additional filter fields

Another feature of the filter panel is that it allows you to add an filter on fields that are not necessarily on the form right now.

How to do it...

To do this, click on the Add a filter field link at the bottom of the list of filter fields.

Then when the list of available fields is displayed, scroll down and find the field that you want to filter on and (like the Currency field) then select it.

Now you will see that the field had been added to the list of fields that you can filter on.

If you use the dropdown search on the filter you will see any valid records or you can just type in the filter that you want to apply to the form.

After you have updated your filter criteria, just click on the Apply button.

Now you will see that the list page has been filtered for you.

daxc   www.dynamicsaxcompanions.com
Dynamics AX Companions
- 173 -
www.blindsquirrelpublishing.com
© 2015 Blind Squirrel Publishing, LLC , All Rights Reserved
 BLIND SQUIRREL PUBLISHING

Adding additional filter fields

How to do it…

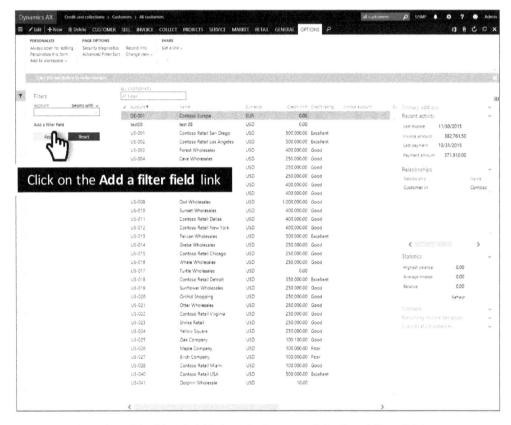

To do this, click on the Add a filter field link at the bottom of the list of filter fields.

daxc www.dynamicsaxcompanions.com
Dynamics AX Companions
- 174 -
www.blindsquirrelpublishing.com
© 2015 Blind Squirrel Publishing, LLC , All Rights Reserved
BLIND SQUIRREL PUBLISHING

Adding additional filter fields

How to do it...

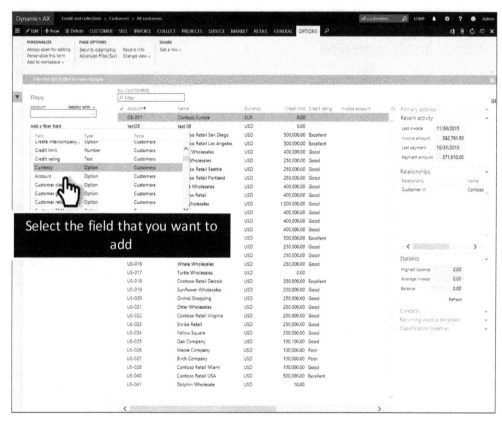

Then when the list of available fields is displayed, scroll down and find the field that you want to filter on and (like the Currency field) then select it.

Adding additional filter fields

How to do it…

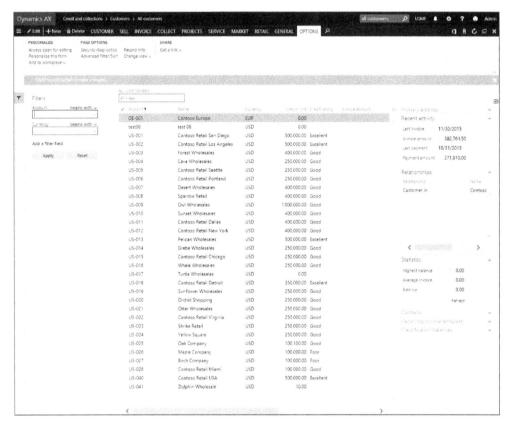

Now you will see that the field had been added to the list of fields that you can filter on.

 www.dynamicsaxcompanions.com
Dynamics AX Companions
- 176 -
www.blindsquirrelpublishing.com
© 2015 Blind Squirrel Publishing, LLC , All Rights Reserved
BLIND SQUIRREL PUBLISHING

Adding additional filter fields

How to do it...

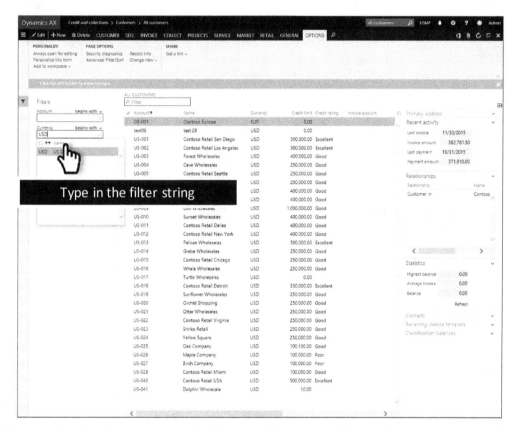

If you use the dropdown search on the filter you will see any valid records or you can just type in the filter that you want to apply to the form.

daxc www.dynamicsaxcompanions.com
Dynamics AX Companions

- 177 -

www.blindsquirrelpublishing.com
© 2015 Blind Squirrel Publishing, LLC , All Rights Reserved

BLIND SQUIRREL PUBLISHING

Adding additional filter fields

How to do it…

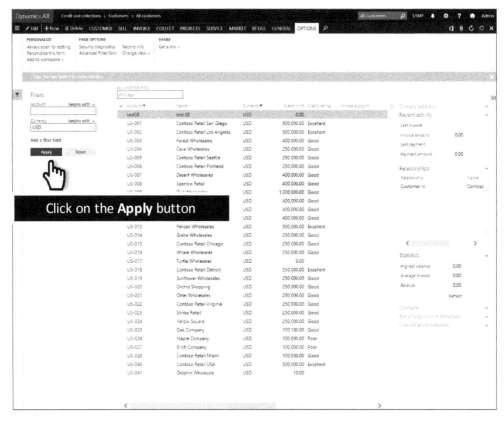

After you have updated your filter criteria, just click on the Apply button.

daxc www.dynamicsaxcompanions.com
Dynamics AX Companions

- 178 -

www.blindsquirrelpublishing.com
© 2015 Blind Squirrel Publishing, LLC , All Rights Reserved

BLIND SQUIRREL
PUBLISHING

Adding additional filter fields

How to do it…

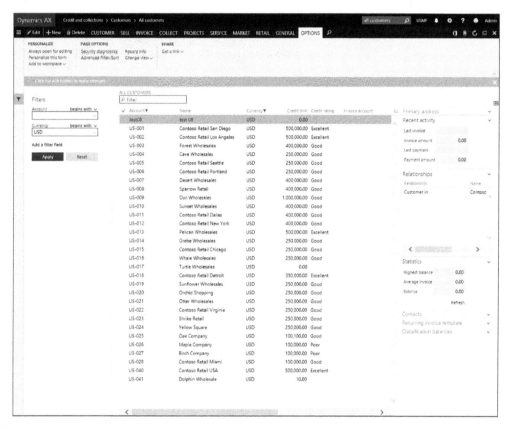

Now you will see that the list page has been filtered for you.

Using the advanced filter

There is one final filter tool that you can take advantage of within the forms, and this is the Advanced filter/sort. If anyone has used prior versions of Dynamics AX, then this is very similar to the advanced filter that was available in those versions.

How to do it...

You access this feature by first clicking on the Options tab in the ribbon bar.

And then you will be able to select the Advanced Filter/Sort from the Page Options group.

This will open up a dialog pane on the right hand side of the form that has all of the default filters for this form.

If you want to filter on a field that is not already on the filter field list then just click on the Add button.

This will add a new filter line to the list of fields that you can filter on.

Just click on the dropdown list for the Field and select the field that you want to filter on – like the Credit Limit field.

Now you will have an additional filter cirteria.

Now you can type in the filter criteria. Note that this allows you to use more advanced filters including wild cards (*), comparison operators (>, <, =) and also placeholders (?) to refine your query even more.

When you are done just click on the OK button.

Now the list page will be filtered based on the advanced query.

As a side note, if you open up the filter panel on the left then you will see that the criteria that you entered in within the Advanced filter is now the default filter there as well.

Using the advanced filter

How to do it…

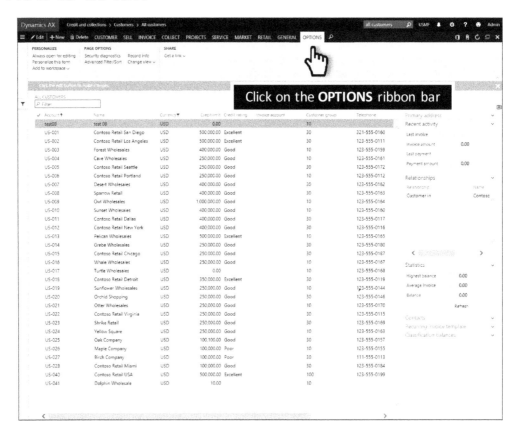

You access this feature by first clicking on the Options tab in the ribbon bar.

Using the advanced filter

How to do it…

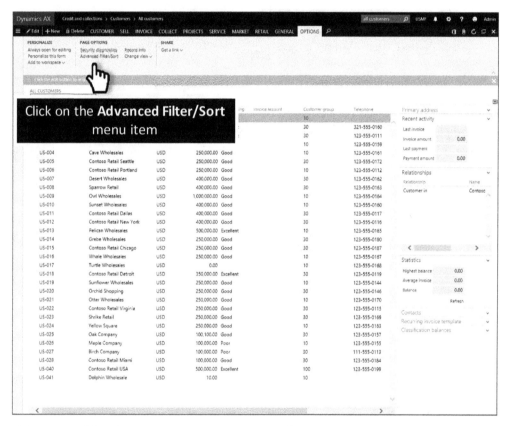

And then you will be able to select the Advanced Filter/Sort from the Page Options group.

daxc   www.dynamicsaxcompanions.com
Dynamics AX Companions

- 183 -

www.blindsquirrelpublishing.com
© 2015 Blind Squirrel Publishing, LLC , All Rights Reserved

BLIND SQUIRREL
PUBLISHING

Using the advanced filter

How to do it…

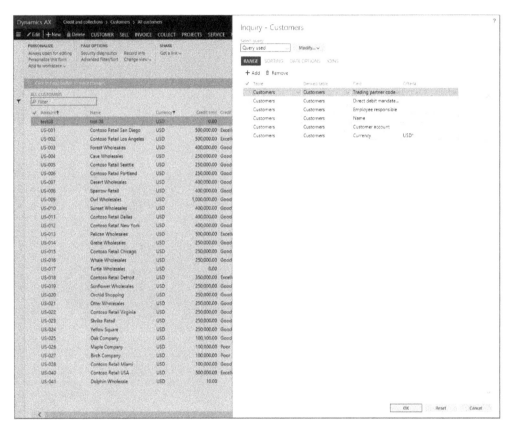

This will open up a dialog pane on the right hand side of the form that has all of the default filters for this form.

daxc   www.dynamicsaxcompanions.com
Dynamics AX Companions
- 184 -
www.blindsquirrelpublishing.com
© 2015 Blind Squirrel Publishing, LLC, All Rights Reserved
BLIND SQUIRREL
PUBLISHING

Using the advanced filter

How to do it…

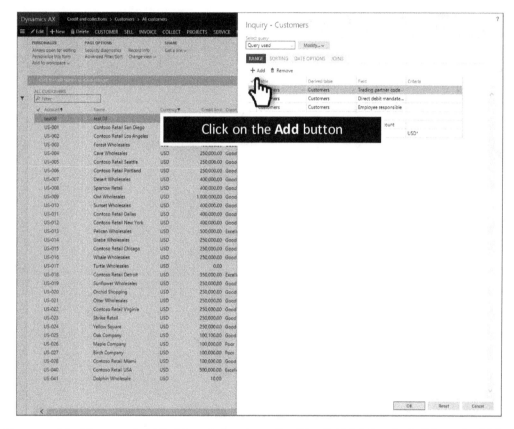

If you want to filter on a field that is not already on the filter field list then just click on the Add button.

Using the advanced filter

How to do it…

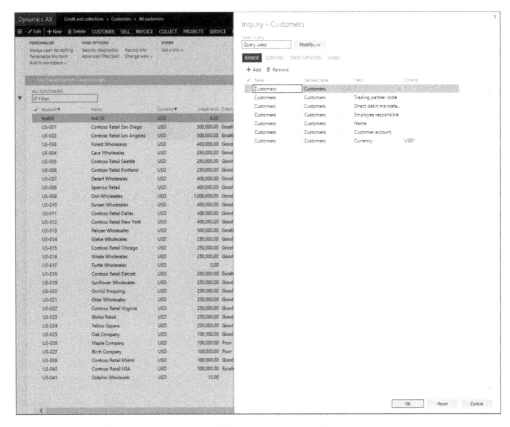

This will add a new filter line to the list of fields that you can filter on.

daxc www.dynamicsaxcompanions.com
Dynamics AX Companions
- 186 -
www.blindsquirrelpublishing.com
© 2015 Blind Squirrel Publishing, LLC , All Rights Reserved
BLIND SQUIRREL
PUBLISHING

Using the advanced filter

How to do it…

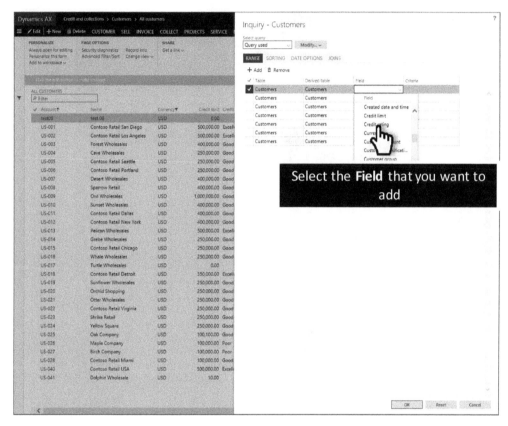

Just click on the dropdown list for the Field and select the field that you want to filter on – like the Credit Limit field.

- 187 -

Using the advanced filter

How to do it…

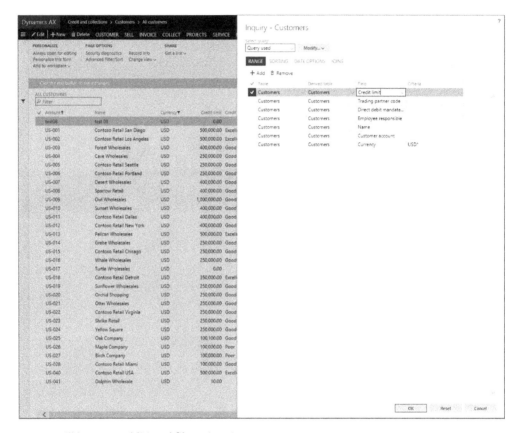

Now you will have an additional filter cirteria.

Using the advanced filter

How to do it…

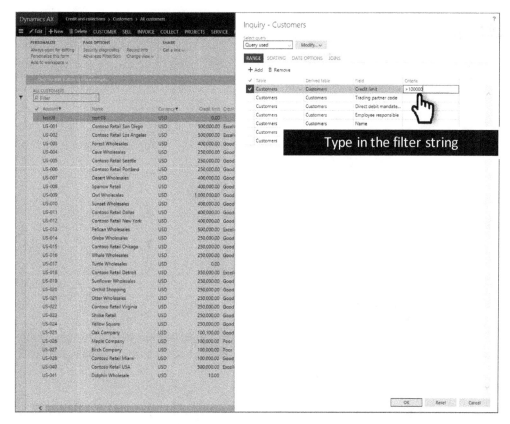

Now you can type in the filter criteria. Note that this allows you to use more advanced filters including wild cards (*), comparison operators (>, <, =) and also placeholders (?) to refine your query even more.

daxc   www.dynamicsaxcompanions.com
Dynamics AX Companions

- 189 -

www.blindsquirrelpublishing.com
© 2015 Blind Squirrel Publishing, LLC , All Rights Reserved

BLIND SQUIRREL
PUBLISHING

Using the advanced filter

How to do it...

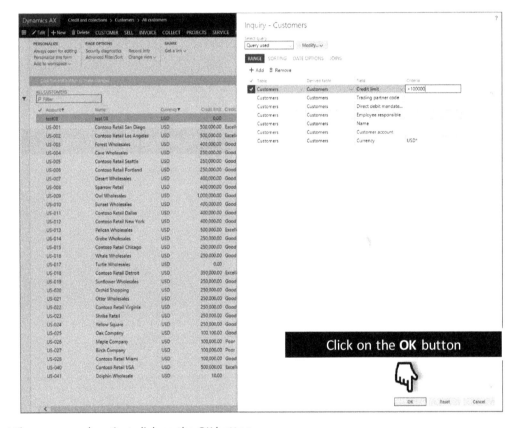

When you are done just click on the OK button.

da✕c www.dynamicsaxcompanions.com
Dynamics AX Companions
- 190 -
www.blindsquirrelpublishing.com
© 2015 Blind Squirrel Publishing, LLC , All Rights Reserved
BLIND SQUIRREL
PUBLISHING

Using the advanced filter

How to do it...

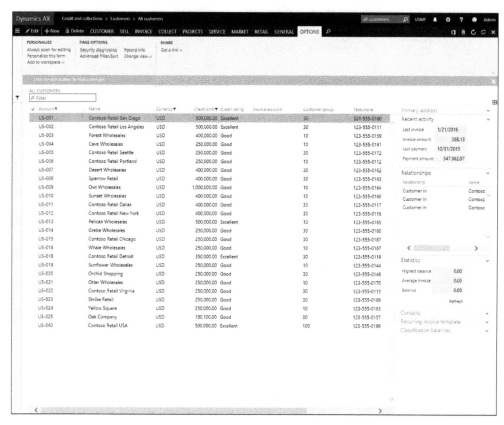

Now the list page will be filtered based on the advanced query.

Using the advanced filter

How to do it…

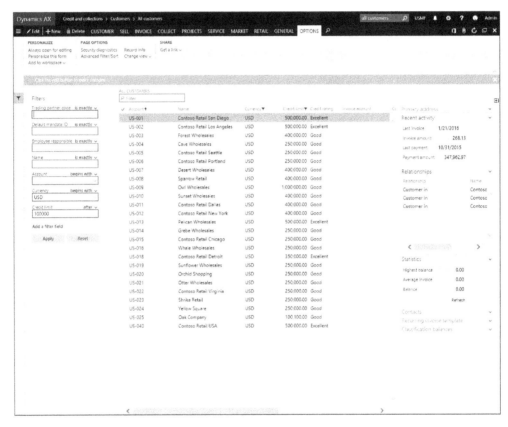

As a side note, if you open up the filter panel on the left then you will see that the criteria that you entered in within the Advanced filter is now the default filter there as well.

daxc
www.dynamicsaxcompanions.com
Dynamics AX Companions

- 192 -

www.blindsquirrelpublishing.com
© 2015 Blind Squirrel Publishing, LLC , All Rights Reserved

BLIND SQUIRREL
PUBLISHING

Adding A Filter To A Workspace As A Tile

If you don't want to have to recreate your filters every time that you want to see particular data, then there is a cool feature within Dynamics AX that allows you to save your filters as tiles within your workspaces so that you can access them quickly and without any more work.

How to do it...

To do this, start off by selecting the OPTIONS action panel.

Then click on the Add to Workspace menu item

Now click on the Workspace dropdown list and you will see a list of all of the workspaces. Select the one that you want to add the tile to.

Now click on the Presentation dropdown list and select the Tile option.

And then click on the Configure button.

This will open up a new dialog panel for you with some extra information about the tile that you want to add.

If you like you can change the Name on Tile field to make the tile a little more descriptive.

And when you are done, click on the OK button to create the tile.

Now when you go to the workspace that you just added the tile to then you will see that it is there, waiting for you to click on it.

 www.dynamicsaxcompanions.com
Dynamics AX Companions

- 193 -

www.blindsquirrelpublishing.com
© 2015 Blind Squirrel Publishing, LLC , All Rights Reserved

BLIND SQUIRREL
PUBLISHING

Adding A Filter To A Workspace As A Tile

How to do it…

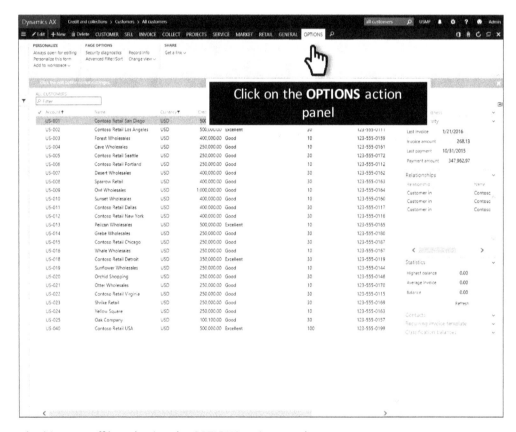

To do this, start off by selecting the OPTIONS action panel.

daxc www.dynamicsaxcompanions.com
Dynamics AX Companions
- 194 -
www.blindsquirrelpublishing.com
© 2015 Blind Squirrel Publishing, LLC , All Rights Reserved
 BLIND SQUIRREL PUBLISHING

Adding A Filter To A Workspace As A Tile

How to do it...

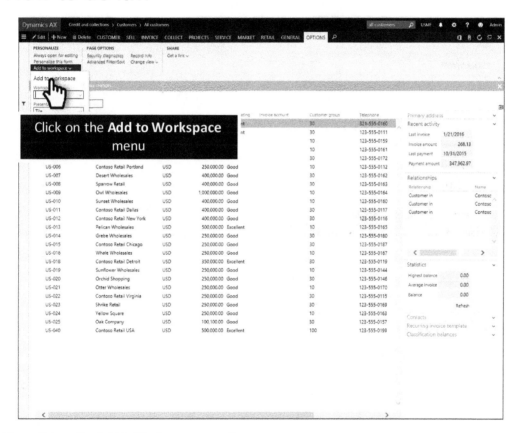

Then click on the Add to Workspace menu item

Adding A Filter To A Workspace As A Tile

How to do it…

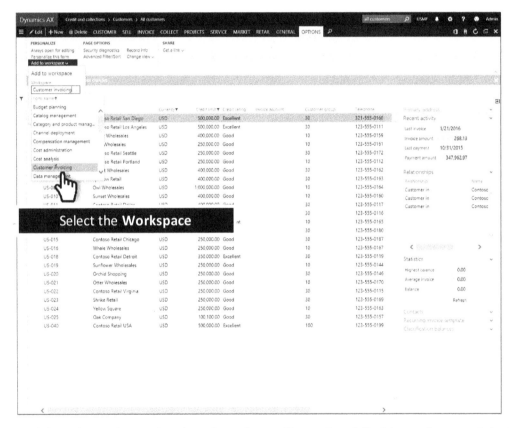

Now click on the Workspace dropdown list and you will see a list of all of the workspaces. Select the one that you want to add the tile to.

daxc   www.dynamicsaxcompanions.com
Dynamics AX Companions

- 196 -

www.blindsquirrelpublishing.com
© 2015 Blind Squirrel Publishing, LLC , All Rights Reserved

BLIND SQUIRREL
PUBLISHING

Adding A Filter To A Workspace As A Tile

How to do it…

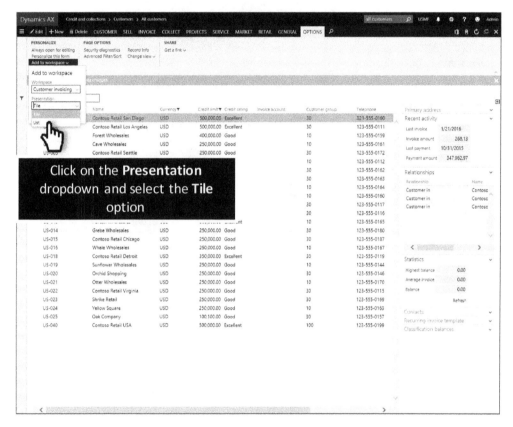

Now click on the Presentation dropdown list and select the Tile option.

Adding A Filter To A Workspace As A Tile

How to do it…

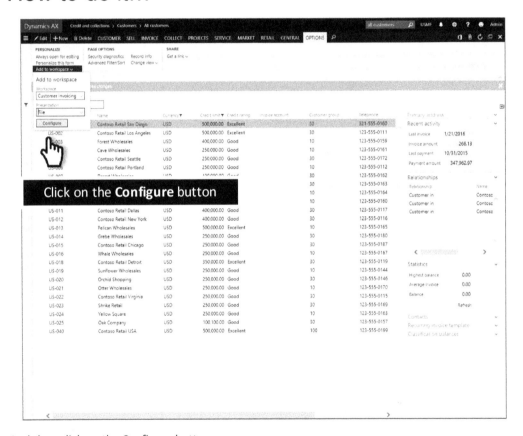

And then click on the Configure button.

www.dynamicsaxcompanions.com
Dynamics AX Companions
- 198 -
www.blindsquirrelpublishing.com
© 2015 Blind Squirrel Publishing, LLC , All Rights Reserved
BLIND SQUIRREL
PUBLISHING

Adding A Filter To A Workspace As A Tile

How to do it...

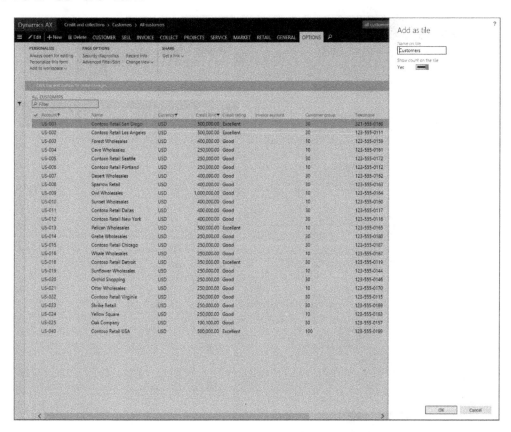

This will open up a new dialog panel for you with some extra information about the tile that you want to add.

Adding A Filter To A Workspace As A Tile

How to do it…

If you like you can change the Name on Tile field to make the tile a little more descriptive.

www.dynamicsaxcompanions.com
Dynamics AX Companions

- 200 -

www.blindsquirrelpublishing.com
© 2015 Blind Squirrel Publishing, LLC , All Rights Reserved

BLIND SQUIRREL PUBLISHING

Adding A Filter To A Workspace As A Tile

How to do it…

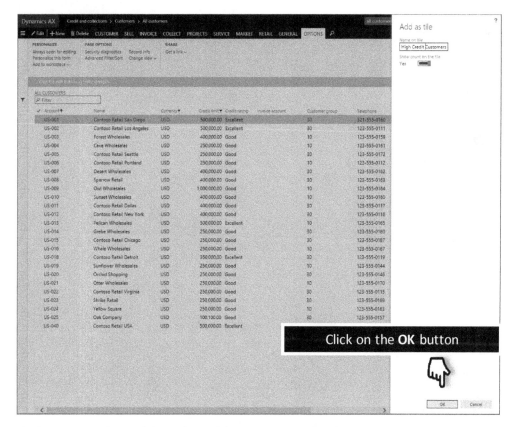

And when you are done, click on the OK button to create the tile.

da𝑥c www.dynamicsaxcompanions.com
Dynamics AX Companions

- 201 -

www.blindsquirrelpublishing.com
© 2015 Blind Squirrel Publishing, LLC , All Rights Reserved

BLIND SQUIRREL
PUBLISHING

Adding A Filter To A Workspace As A Tile

How to do it…

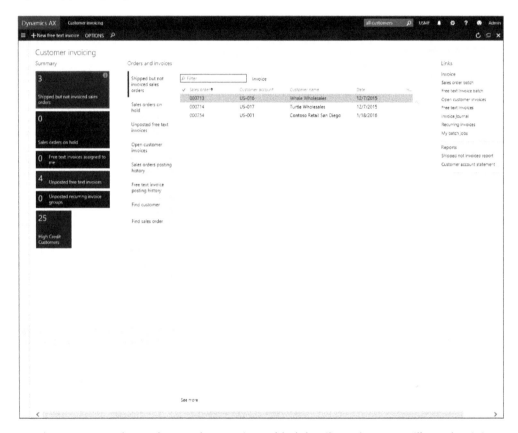

Now when you go to the workspace that you just added the tile to then you will see that it is there, waiting for you to click on it.

Adding A Tile To The Default Dashboard

The usefulness of the tiles does not stop there. There is another feature that you may want to take advantage of and that is to add the summary from the tile to the default dashboard menu. This gives you an even easier way to navigate to just the data that you need.

How to do it...

To do this, right-mouse-click on the tile that you want to add to the dashboard and then select the Personalize option from the context menu.

This will open up a personalization pop-up box.

All you need to do here is check the Pin to Dashboard option within the personalization.

Now when you go back to your default dashboard you will see that there is a summary from the tile under the workspace link which will take you right to the form with the custom filter.

 www.dynamicsaxcompanions.com
Dynamics AX Companions

- 203 -

www.blindsquirrelpublishing.com
© 2015 Blind Squirrel Publishing, LLC , All Rights Reserved
 BLIND SQUIRREL PUBLISHING

Adding A Tile To The Default Dashboard

How to do it...

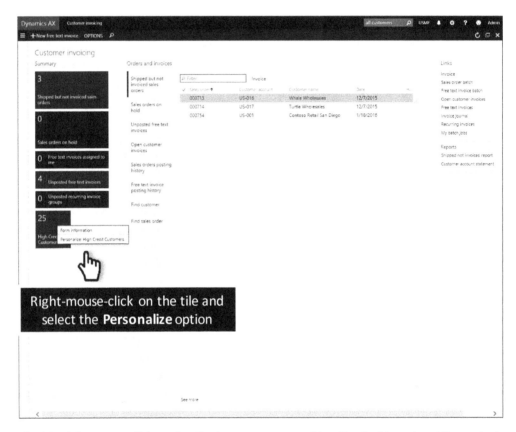

To do this, right-mouse-click on the tile that you want to add to the dashboard and then select the Personalize option from the context menu.

Adding A Tile To The Default Dashboard

How to do it…

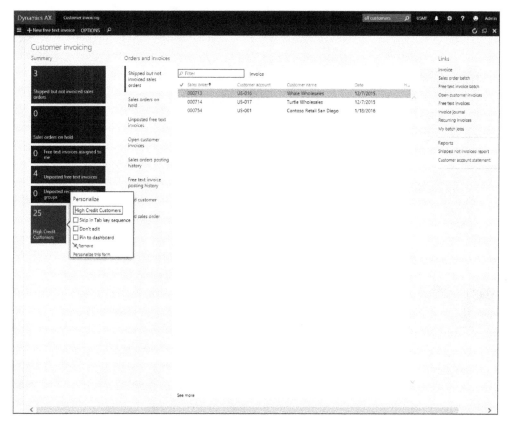

This will open up a personalization pop-up box.

daxc   www.dynamicsaxcompanions.com
Dynamics AX Companions
- 205 -
www.blindsquirrelpublishing.com
© 2015 Blind Squirrel Publishing, LLC , All Rights Reserved
BLIND SQUIRREL
PUBLISHING

Adding A Tile To The Default Dashboard

How to do it…

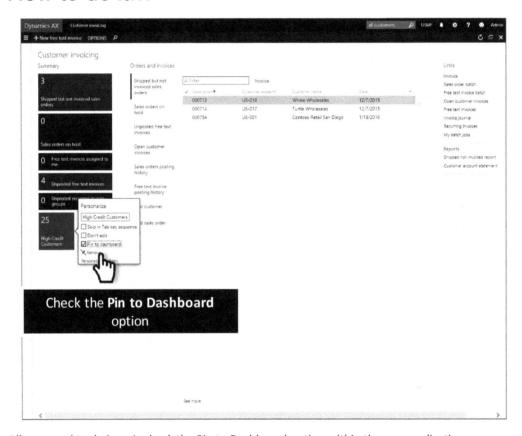

All you need to do here is check the Pin to Dashboard option within the personalization.

daxc
www.dynamicsaxcompanions.com
Dynamics AX Companions

- 206 -

www.blindsquirrelpublishing.com
© 2015 Blind Squirrel Publishing, LLC , All Rights Reserved

BLIND SQUIRREL
PUBLISHING

Adding A Tile To The Default Dashboard

How to do it...

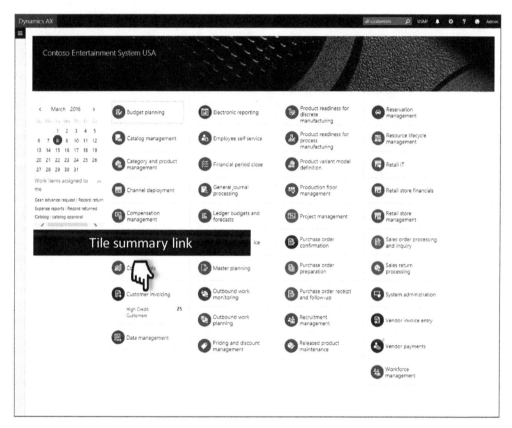

Now when you go back to your default dashboard you will see that there is a summary from the tile under the workspace link which will take you right to the form with the custom filter.

Adding A Filter To A Workspace As A List

There is one other option that you have with the filtered data that you may want to take advantage of and that is the feature that allows you to save your filter as a list panel within the workspaces. This allows you to access the queries directly from the workspaces, making them even more useful.

How to do it...

To do this, start off by selecting the OPTIONS action panel.

Then click on the Add to Workspace menu item

Now click on the Workspace dropdown list and you will see a list of all of the workspaces. Select the one that you want to add the tile to.

Now click on the Presentation dropdown list and select the List option.

And then click on the Configure button.

This will open up a new dialog panel for you with some extra information about the tile that you want to add.

If you like you can change the Name on Tile field to make the tile a little more descriptive.

And when you are done, click on the OK button to create the tile.

Now when you go to the workspace that you just added the list to you will see that it is now displayed within the list section.

Adding A Filter To A Workspace As A List

How to do it…

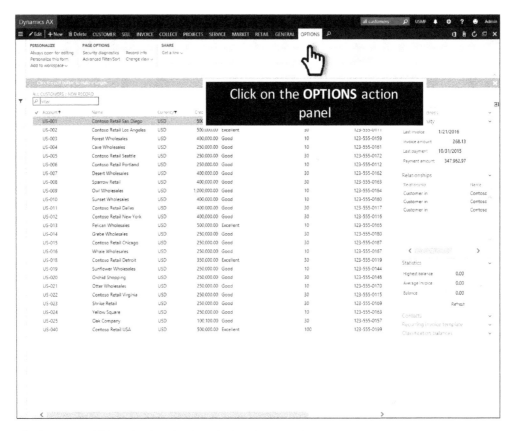

To do this, start off by selecting the OPTIONS action panel.

Adding A Filter To A Workspace As A List

How to do it…

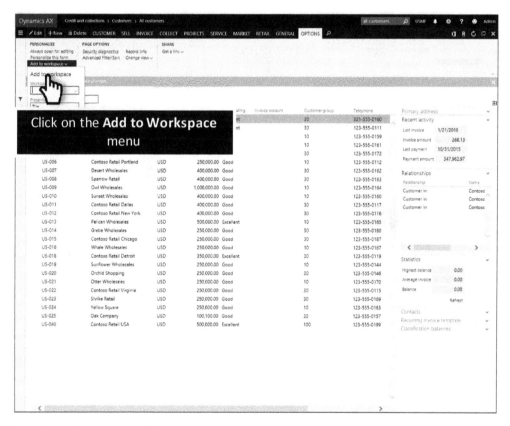

Then click on the Add to Workspace menu item

da✕c   www.dynamicsaxcompanions.com
Dynamics AX Companions

- 211 -

www.blindsquirrelpublishing.com
© 2015 Blind Squirrel Publishing, LLC , All Rights Reserved

BLIND SQUIRREL
PUBLISHING

Adding A Filter To A Workspace As A List

How to do it...

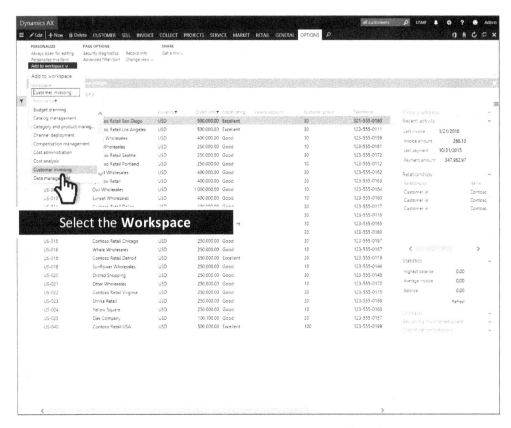

Now click on the Workspace dropdown list and you will see a list of all of the workspaces. Select the one that you want to add the tile to.

daxc   www.dynamicsaxcompanions.com
Dynamics AX Companions

- 212 -

www.blindsquirrelpublishing.com
© 2015 Blind Squirrel Publishing, LLC , All Rights Reserved

BLIND SQUIRREL
PUBLISHING

Adding A Filter To A Workspace As A List

How to do it...

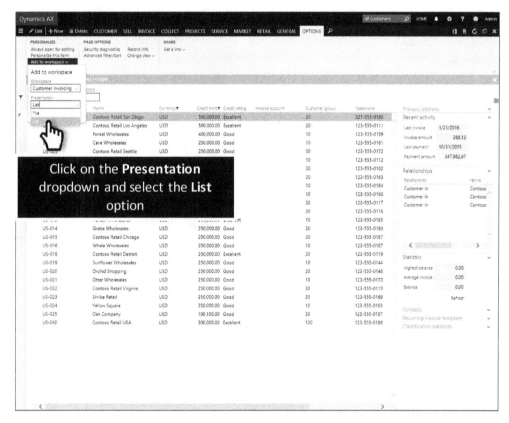

Now click on the Presentation dropdown list and select the List option.

Adding A Filter To A Workspace As A List

How to do it…

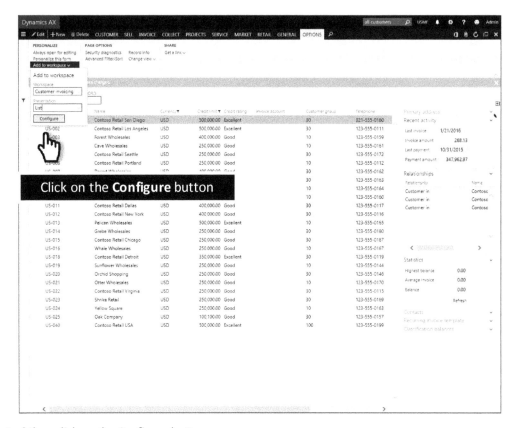

And then click on the Configure button.

Adding A Filter To A Workspace As A List

How to do it…

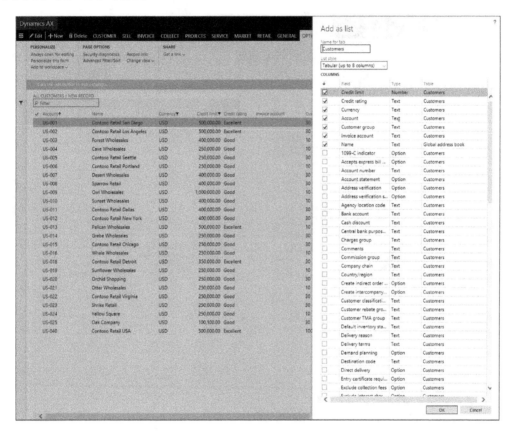

This will open up a new dialog panel for you with some extra information about the tile that you want to add.

Adding A Filter To A Workspace As A List

How to do it…

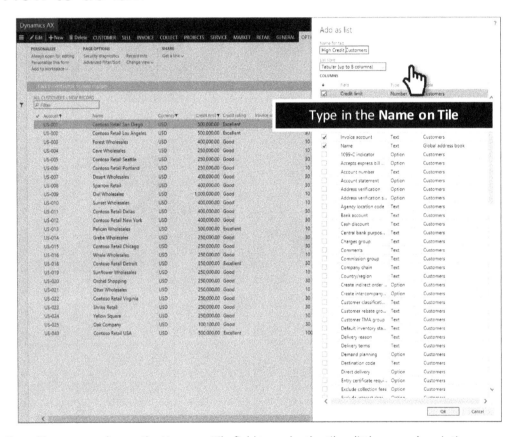

If you like you can change the Name on Tile field to make the tile a little more descriptive.

Adding A Filter To A Workspace As A List

How to do it…

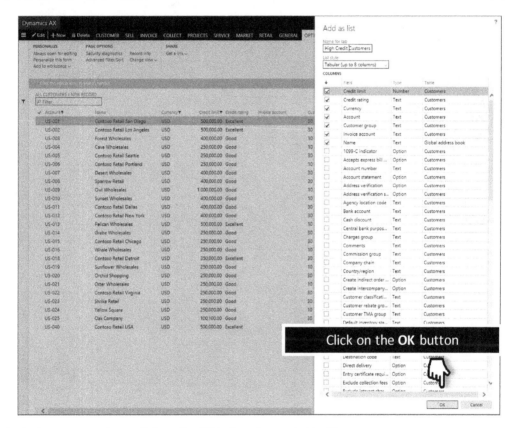

And when you are done, click on the OK button to create the tile.

Adding A Filter To A Workspace As A List

How to do it…

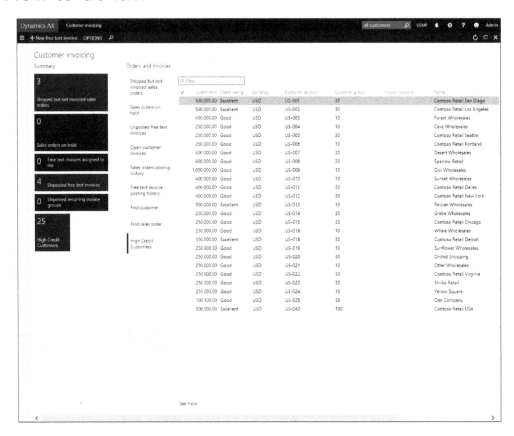

Now when you go to the workspace that you just added the list to you will see that it is now displayed within the list section.

daxc www.dynamicsaxcompanions.com
Dynamics AX Companions

- 218 -

www.blindsquirrelpublishing.com
© 2015 Blind Squirrel Publishing, LLC , All Rights Reserved

 BLIND SQUIRREL PUBLISHING

Exporting to Excel

Another strong feature within the new Dynamics AX is the ability to export the data on a screen out to Excel, update the data and then publish it back to the database.

How to do it...

To do this, just click on the Office button in the top right hand corner of the application.

Then the Office dropdown list is displayed, click on the form name under the OPEN IN EXCEL group.

When the Open in Excel dialog panel is displayed, click on the Download button.

This will create an Excel file for you and if you are asked, click on the Open button in the dialog box.

If this is the first time that you are using the add-in then it will pop up with a request for you to trust it and install it within Excel. Just click on the Trust this add-in button.

If there is an update to the add in then it will also ask you to upgrade. Just click on the Upgrade button.

Finally if you haven't done so already, then the add-in will ask you to authenticate to make sure that you have access to the data. All you need to do here is click on the Sign in link and follow the sign in instructions if there are any.

This will take you into Excel and you will have a Microsoft Dynamics Agave panel on the right hand side of the spreadsheet.

Now go to the cell that you want to change – like the Customer Group in this example.

And then change the value.

To update Dynamics AX, just click on the Publish button in the Dynamics AX panel.

The system will then update the database (if there are no inconsistencies with the data) and tell you that the publishing was successful. Now you can just close Excel.

When you return back to Dynamics AX, you will still see that the data has not been changed. Although this is because you need to click on the Refresh icon in the top right hand corner of the application.

After the form refreshes you will now see that the data has been updated for you.

Exporting to Excel

How to do it…

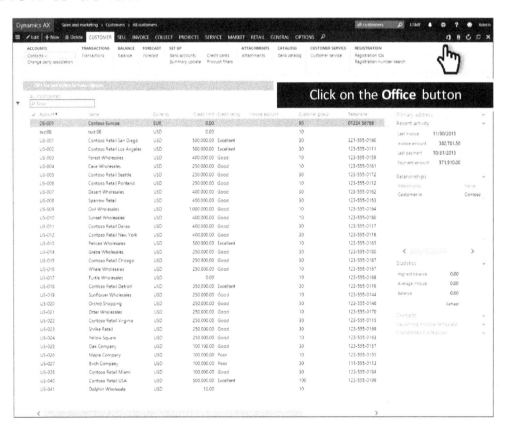

To do this, just click on the Office button in the top right hand corner of the application.

Exporting to Excel

How to do it…

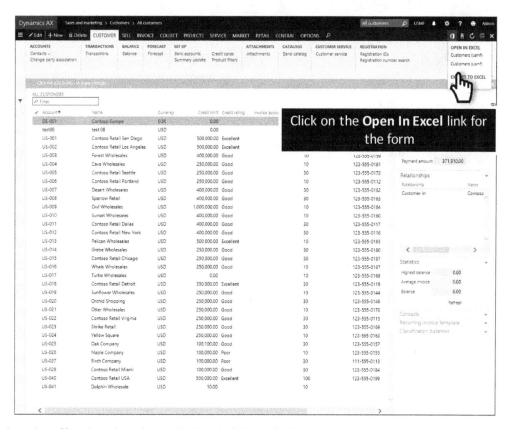

Click on the **Open In Excel** link for the form

Then the Office dropdown list is displayed, click on the form name under the OPEN IN EXCEL group.

daxc   www.dynamicsaxcompanions.com
Dynamics AX Companions
- 221 -
www.blindsquirrelpublishing.com
© 2015 Blind Squirrel Publishing, LLC , All Rights Reserved

BLIND SQUIRREL
PUBLISHING

Exporting to Excel

How to do it…

When the Open in Excel dialog panel is displayed, click on the Download button.

Exporting to Excel

How to do it…

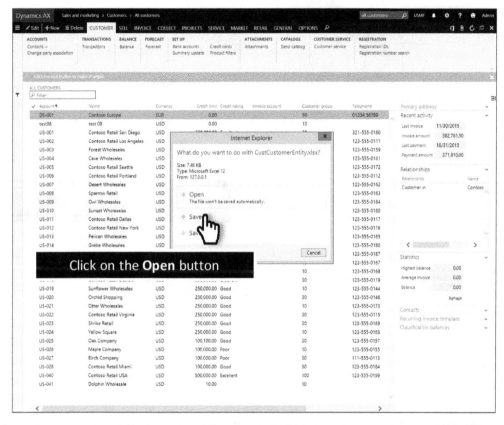

This will create an Excel file for you and if you are asked, click on the Open button in the dialog box.

Exporting to Excel

How to do it…

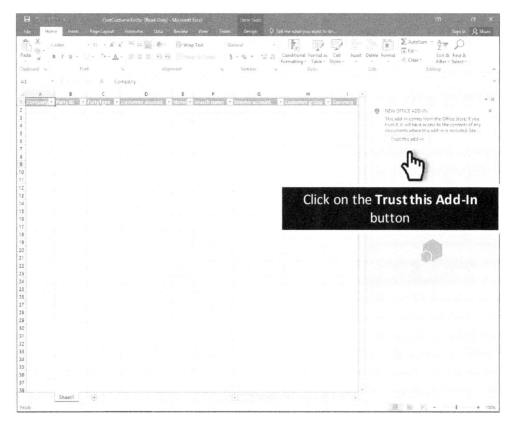

If this is the first time that you are using the add-in then it will pop up with a request for you to trust it and install it within Excel. Just click on the Trust this add-in button.

Exporting to Excel

How to do it…

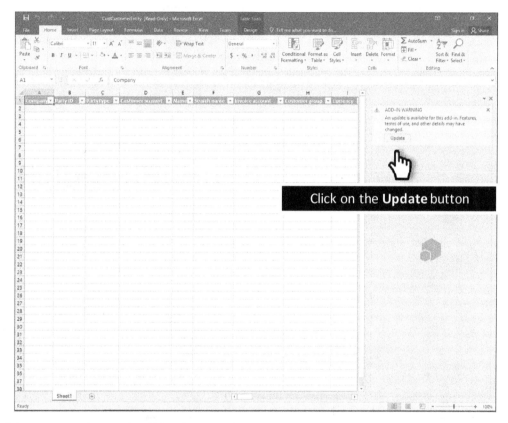

If there is an update to the add in then it will also ask you to upgrade. Just click on the Upgrade button.

Exporting to Excel

How to do it...

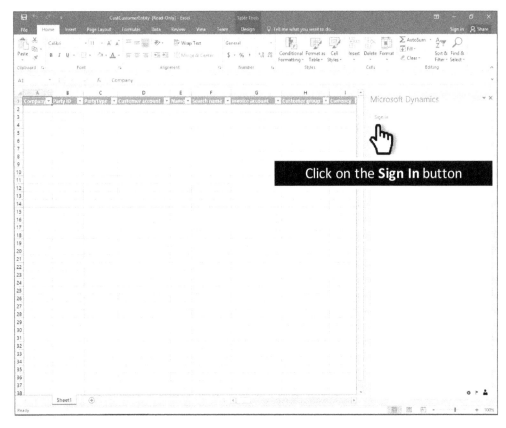

Finally if you haven't done so already, then the add-in will ask you to authenticate to make sure that you have access to the data. All you need to do here is click on the Sign in link and follow the sign in instructions if there are any.

Exporting to Excel

How to do it…

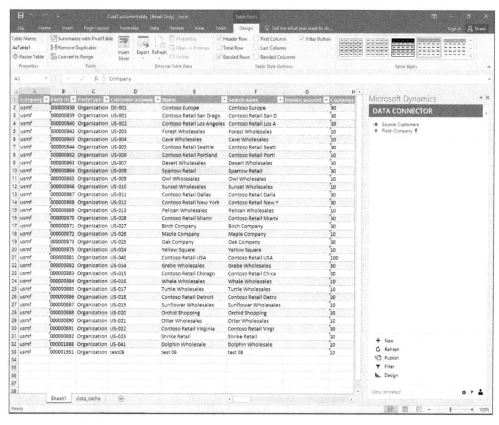

This will take you into Excel and you will have a Microsoft Dynamics Agave panel on the right hand side of the spreadsheet.

Exporting to Excel

How to do it...

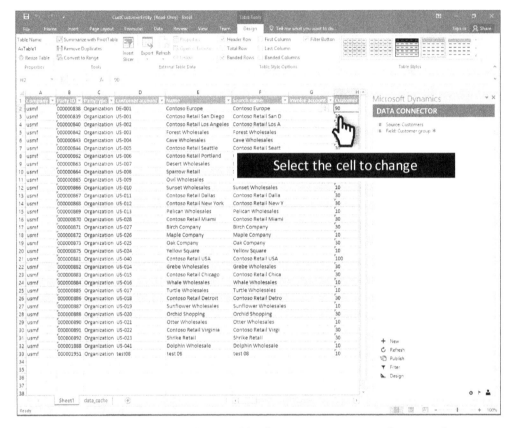

Now go to the cell that you want to change – like the Customer Group in this example.

Exporting to Excel

How to do it…

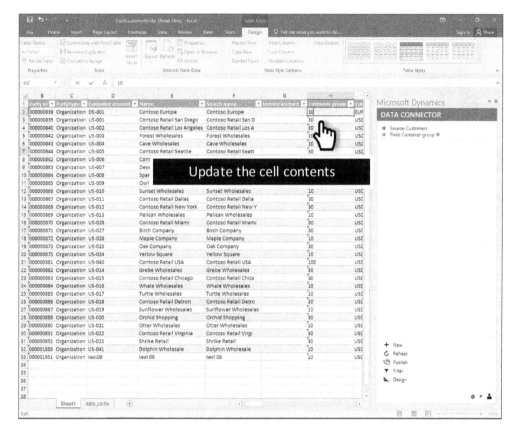

And then change the value.

daxc   www.dynamicsaxcompanions.com
Dynamics AX Companions
- 229 -
www.blindsquirrelpublishing.com
© 2015 Blind Squirrel Publishing, LLC , All Rights Reserved
BLIND SQUIRREL
PUBLISHING

Exporting to Excel

How to do it…

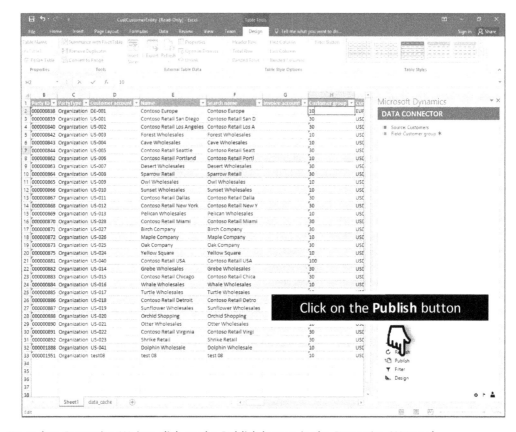

To update Dynamics AX, just click on the Publish button in the Dynamics AX panel.

Exporting to Excel

How to do it...

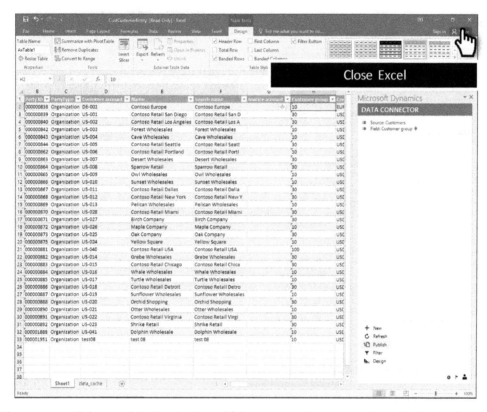

The system will then update the database (if there are no inconsistencies with the data) and tell you that the publishing was successful. Now you can just close Excel.

Exporting to Excel

How to do it…

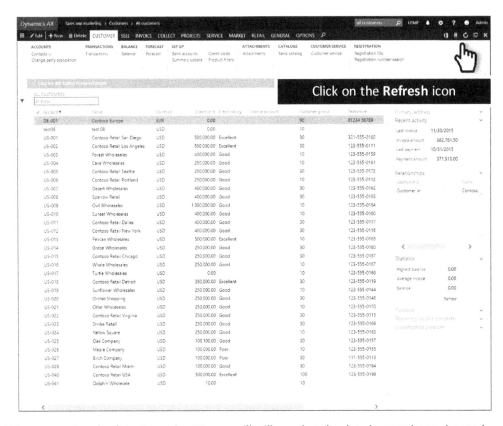

When you return back to Dynamics AX, you will still see that the data has not been changed. Although this is because you need to click on the Refresh icon in the top right hand corner of the application.

daxc   www.dynamicsaxcompanions.com
Dynamics AX Companions
- 232 -
www.blindsquirrelpublishing.com
© 2015 Blind Squirrel Publishing, LLC , All Rights Reserved
BLIND SQUIRREL
PUBLISHING

Exporting to Excel

How to do it...

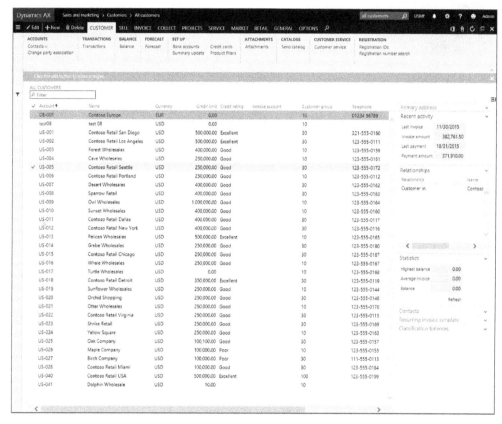

After the form refreshes you will now see that the data has been updated for you.

da✗c   www.dynamicsaxcompanions.com
Dynamics AX Companions
- 233 -
www.blindsquirrelpublishing.com
© 2015 Blind Squirrel Publishing, LLC , All Rights Reserved
 BLIND SQUIRREL
PUBLISHING

The Recent list

As you navigate throughout the day you may want to return back to a form or function that you used earlier on. A quick way to do this is by accessing the Recent list from the hamburger menu.

How to do it...

To see the recent list, click on the Hamburger icon at the top of the form to open up the navigation menu.

And then click on the Recent link within the main menu structure.

To go to any of the previous forms, just click on the link.

Now you will be taken to the form.

www.dynamicsaxcompanions.com
Dynamics AX Companions

- 235 -

www.blindsquirrelpublishing.com
© 2015 Blind Squirrel Publishing, LLC , All Rights Reserved

BLIND SQUIRREL
PUBLISHING

The Recent list

How to do it...

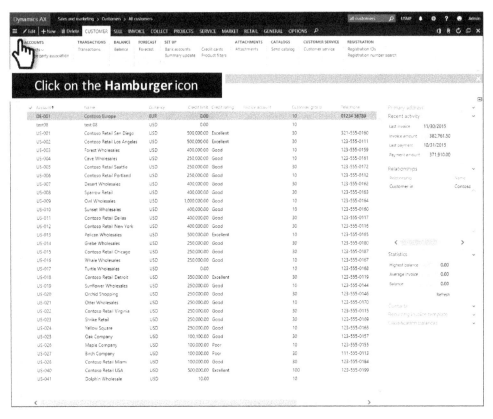

To see the recent list, click on the Hamburger icon at the top of the form to open up the navigation menu.

www.blindsquirrelpublishing.com
© 2015 Blind Squirrel Publishing, LLC , All Rights Reserved

The Recent list

How to do it…

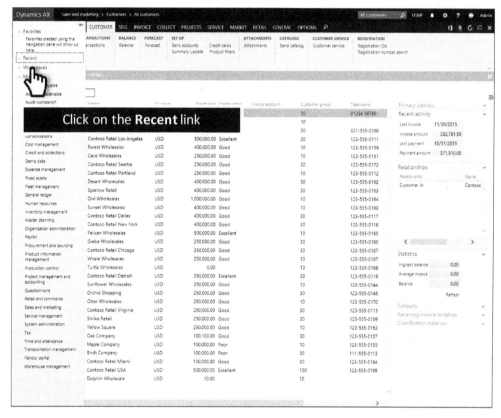

And then click on the Recent link within the main menu structure.

The Recent list

How to do it…

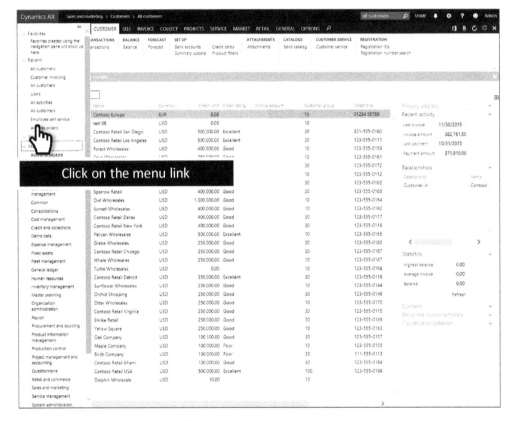

To go to any of the previous forms, just click on the link.

da×c   www.dynamicsaxcompanions.com
       Dynamics AX Companions

- 238 -

www.blindsquirrelpublishing.com
© 2015 Blind Squirrel Publishing, LLC , All Rights Reserved

BLIND SQUIRREL
PUBLISHING

The Recent list

How to do it...

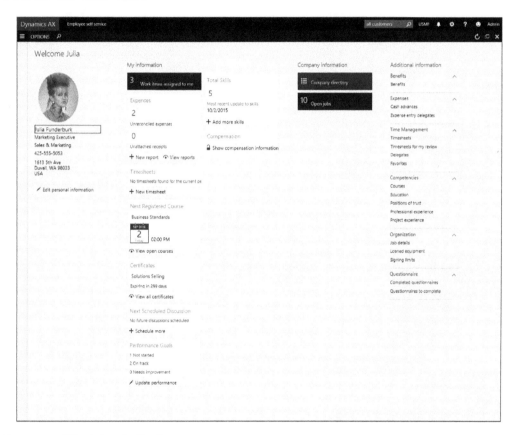

Now you will be taken to the form.

daxc   www.dynamicsaxcompanions.com
        Dynamics AX Companions

        - 239 -

www.blindsquirrelpublishing.com
© 2015 Blind Squirrel Publishing, LLC , All Rights Reserved

BLIND SQUIRREL
PUBLISHING

Adding favorite menu items

Another way that you can find the forms that you commonly use is to add them to the Favorites list.

How to do it...

To see the Favorites just click on the Hamburger icon to open up the main menu.

And then click on the Favorites item.

Right now there aren't any favorites within the list so we will add a few.

You can add any menu item to the favorites, but probably you will want to add something that you have already opened so a trick here is to click on the Recent list.

Then just hover over the menu items that you want to add to the favorites and check the favorites Star to the right of the name.

Now when you return back to the Favorites menu you will see that all of the items that you added are there in the favorites list.

da✗c   www.dynamicsaxcompanions.com
Dynamics AX Companions

- 241 -

www.blindsquirrelpublishing.com
© 2015 Blind Squirrel Publishing, LLC , All Rights Reserved

 BLIND SQUIRREL
PUBLISHING

Adding favorite menu items

How to do it…

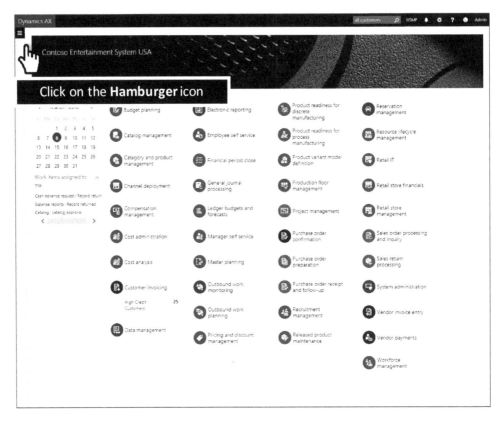

To see the Favorites just click on the Hamburger icon to open up the main menu.

Adding favorite menu items

How to do it...

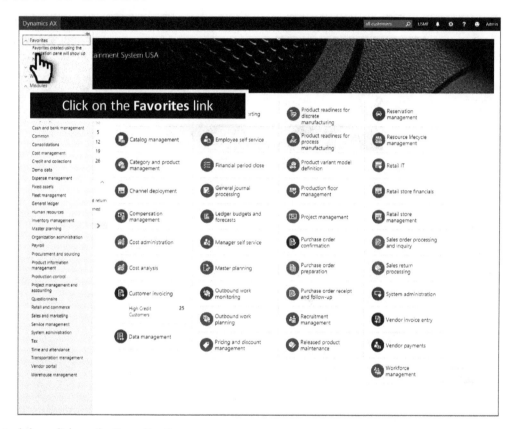

And then click on the Favorites item.

Right now there aren't any favorites within the list so we will add a few.

Adding favorite menu items

How to do it…

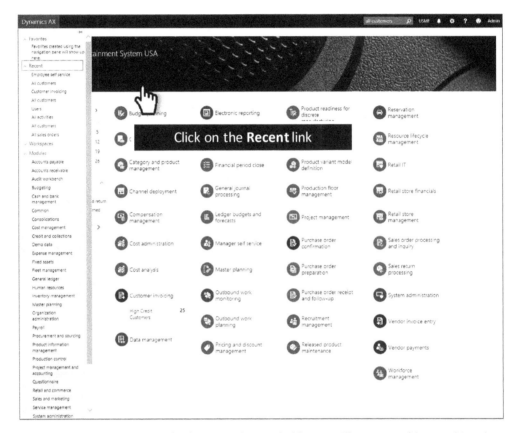

You can add any menu item to the favorites, but probably you will want to add something that you have already opened so a trick here is to click on the Recent list.

Adding favorite menu items

How to do it…

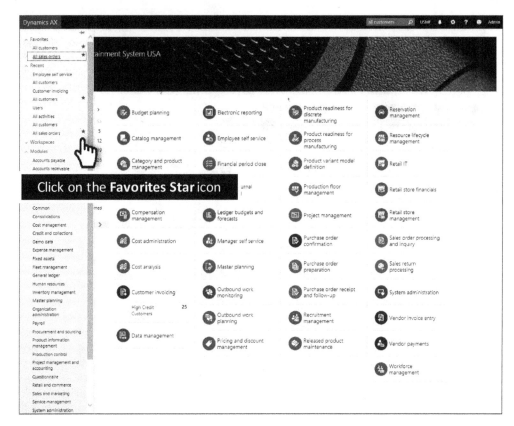

Then just hover over the menu items that you want to add to the favorites and check the favorites Star to the right of the name.

daxc   www.dynamicsaxcompanions.com
       Dynamics AX Companions
       - 245 -
       www.blindsquirrelpublishing.com
       © 2015 Blind Squirrel Publishing, LLC , All Rights Reserved
       BLIND SQUIRREL
       PUBLISHING

Adding favorite menu items

How to do it…

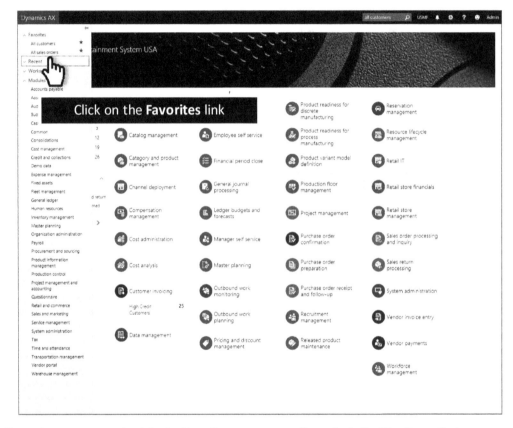

Now when you return back to the Favorites menu you will see that all of the items that you added are there in the favorites list.

www.dynamicsaxcompanions.com
Dynamics AX Companions

- 246 -

www.blindsquirrelpublishing.com
© 2015 Blind Squirrel Publishing, LLC , All Rights Reserved

BLIND SQUIRREL
PUBLISHING

Updating user options

There are a number of personalization options that you can set at the user level which will follow them regardless of where they are logging in from.

How to do it...

To access the user options, click on the Gear icon in the top right of the form.

Then when the menu is displayed, select the Options menu item.

This will take you to the user options and open up the Visual options page and you will see that you can update a lot of things here including the color, the density of the form, and also a number of the defaults for the user interface.

If you click on any of the color swatches then you can change the default color of the application accents. This is not just a fashion statement, it is also a great way to identify different users if you have multiple log ins.

Additionally there is a high contrast swatch that is available as well.

You can choose the one that you like.

Also at the bottom of this form are two density options that you can choose from for displaying the data. If you work on more of a touch based device like a tablet then you may prefer to use the low density option.

If you work on more of a traditional device then you may want to use the high density view.

There are also some regional preferences that you can make as a user here as well that you can access by clicking on the Preferences tab link.

 www.dynamicsaxcompanions.com
Dynamics AX Companions

- 247 -

 www.blindsquirrelpublishing.com
© 2015 Blind Squirrel Publishing, LLC , All Rights Reserved
BLIND SQUIRREL PUBLISHING

One other item to note here on the Preferences page is that you can change your default startup company here by selecting the company from the dropdown list.

If you click on the Default start page dropdown list then you will see that you can change the default start page from the dashboard to the Employee Self Service page, or the Systems Administrator page based on your user preference.

If you want to change the language that you use then just click on the Language dropdown list and select your new preferred language.

After you have selected the language, just refresh the form.

Now you will see that all of the prompts and metadata have been changed to your new language.

After you have reset back to your preferred language, click on the x button in the top right hand corner to exit from the form.

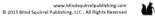

Updating user options

How to do it...

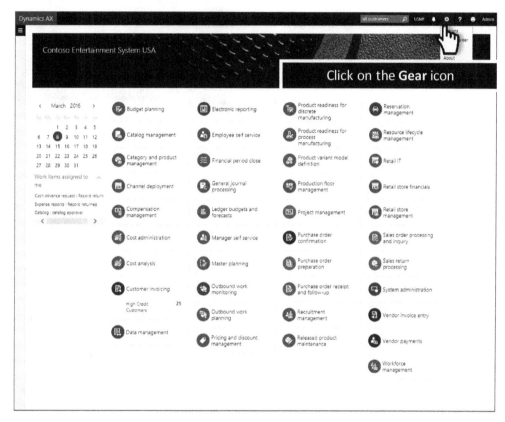

To access the user options, click on the Gear icon in the top right of the form.

Updating user options

How to do it…

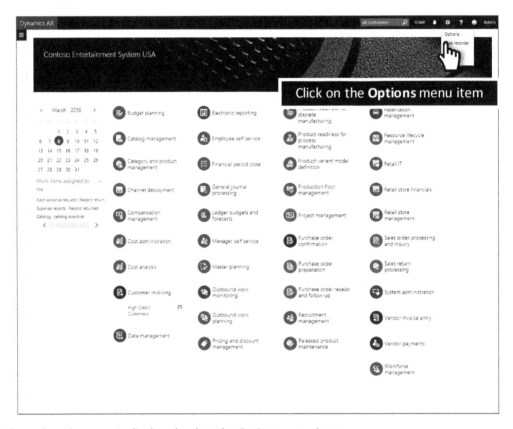

Then when the menu is displayed, select the Options menu item.

daxc   www.dynamicsaxcompanions.com
Dynamics AX Companions
- 250 -
www.blindsquirrelpublishing.com
© 2015 Blind Squirrel Publishing, LLC , All Rights Reserved
BLIND SQUIRREL
PUBLISHING

Updating user options

How to do it…

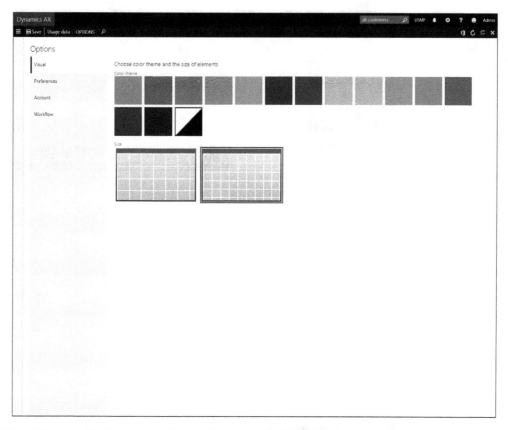

This will take you to the user options and open up the Visual options page and you will see that you can update a lot of things here including the color, the density of the form, and also a number of the defaults for the user interface.

Updating user options

How to do it…

If you click on any of the color swatches then you can change the default color of the application accents. This is not just a fashion statement, it is also a great way to identify different users if you have multiple log ins.

Updating user options

How to do it...

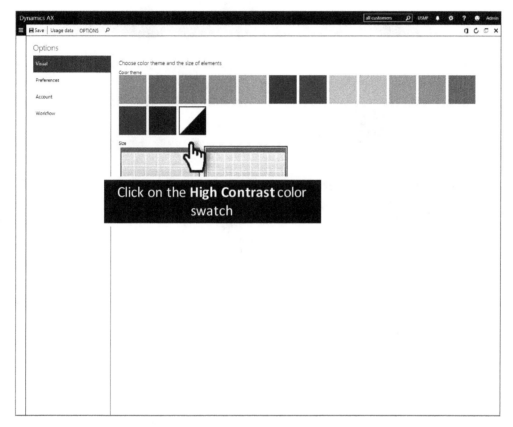

Additionally there is a high contrast swatch that is available as well.

Updating user options

How to do it...

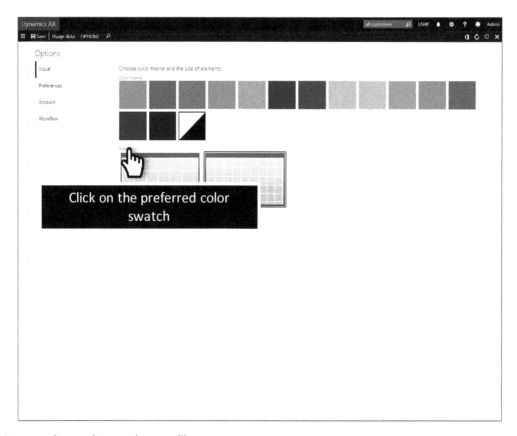

You can choose the one that you like.

Updating user options

How to do it…

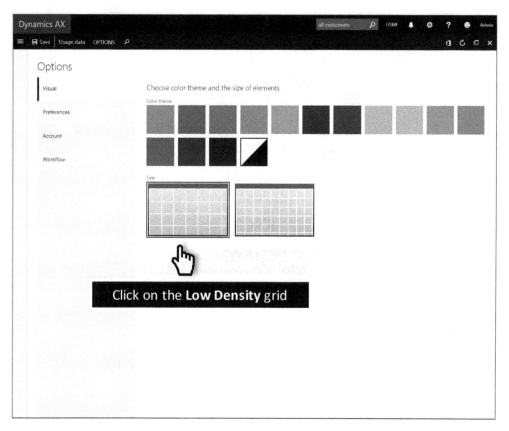

Also at the bottom of this form are two density options that you can choose from for displaying the data. If you work on more of a touch based device like a tablet then you may prefer to use the low density option.

daxc www.dynamicsaxcompanions.com
Dynamics AX Companions

- 255 -

www.blindsquirrelpublishing.com
© 2015 Blind Squirrel Publishing, LLC , All Rights Reserved

BLIND SQUIRREL
PUBLISHING

Updating user options

How to do it…

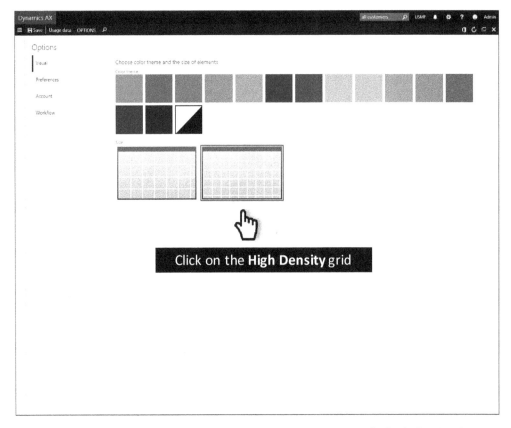

If you work on more of a traditional device then you may want to use the high density view.

Updating user options

How to do it...

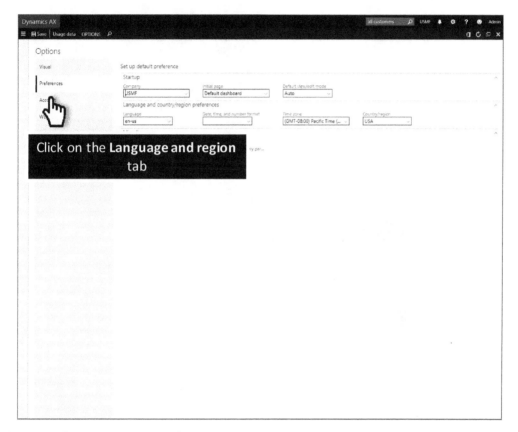

There are also some regional preferences that you can make as a user here as well that you can access by clicking on the Preferences tab link.

Updating user options

How to do it…

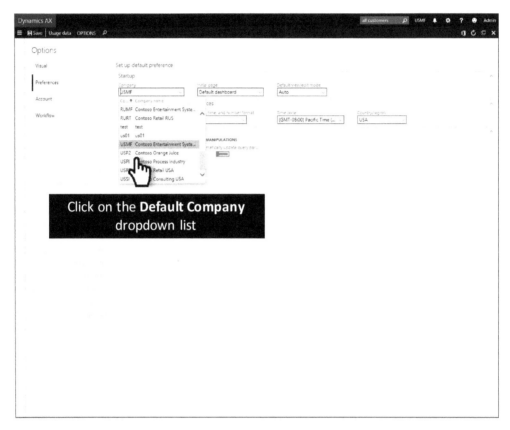

One other item to note here on the Preferences page is that you can change your default startup company here by selecting the company from the dropdown list.

daxc   www.dynamicsaxcompanions.com
Dynamics AX Companions
- 258 -
www.blindsquirrelpublishing.com
© 2015 Blind Squirrel Publishing, LLC , All Rights Reserved
 BLIND SQUIRREL PUBLISHING

Updating user options

How to do it…

If you click on the Default start page dropdown list then you will see that you can change the default start page from the dashboard to the Employee Self Service page, or the Systems Administrator page based on your user preference.

Updating user options

How to do it...

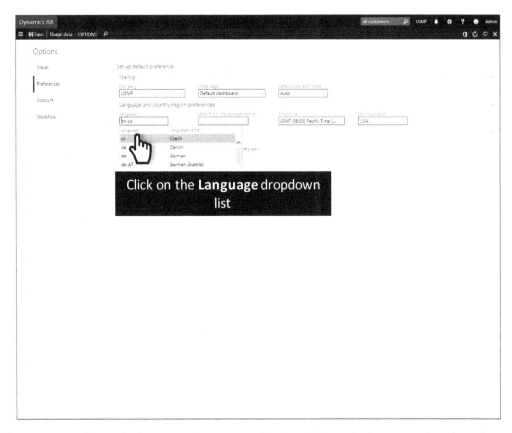

If you want to change the language that you use then just click on the Language dropdown list and select your new preferred language.

Updating user options

How to do it...

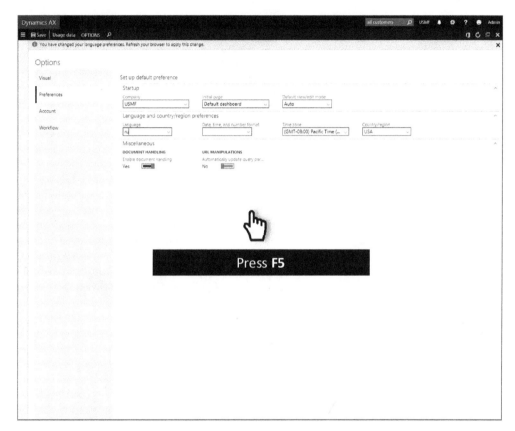

After you have selected the language, just refresh the form.

Updating user options

How to do it…

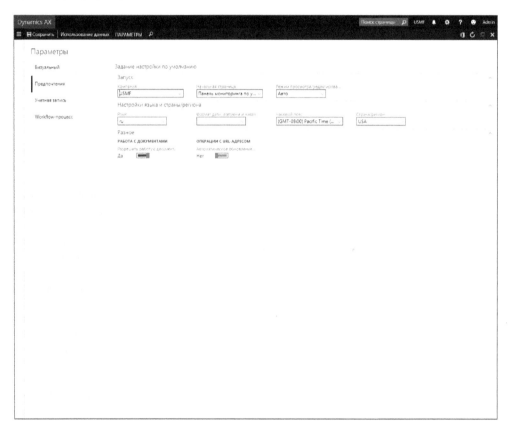

Now you will see that all of the prompts and metadata have been changed to your new language.

Updating user options

How to do it…

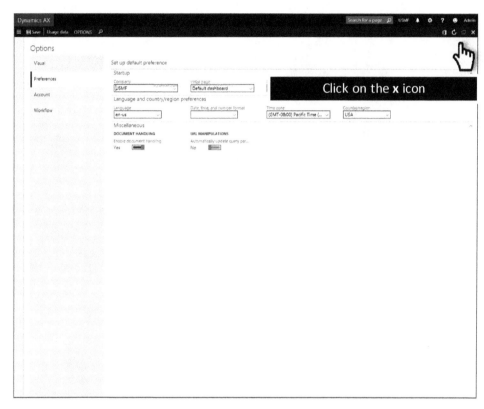

After you have reset back to your preferred language, click on the x button in the top right hand corner to exit from the form.

Entering an order

One of the most important things to consider with an application like the new Dynamics AX is the usability from a data entry point. Even though this is a web based application you don't want to have to use the mouse all of the time in order to enter in transactions, especially in high volume situations. So lets see how you can use the shortcut keys to enter in transactions.

How to do it...

Start off by clicking on the Sales Order Processing and Inquiry workspace tile on the default dashboard.

This will open up the main workspace for order entry.

Now press ALT+N to access the New menu item and then click the DOWN ARROW to see the menu items. From here you can select the Sales Order menu item.

The New Sales Order dialog will now show up on the right hand side of the form.

To select a customer, just type in part of the customer details that you want to search on. If you type in part of the account number then it will show you all of the account numbers that match using the search ahead feature.

If you type in something that is found in some of the other columns – like the name for example then the system is smart enough to match it up to the other columns.

Once you have found the customer just press ENTER to select it and then ENTER again to create the new sales order.

Now you will be in the sales order maintenance form.

da&c   www.dynamicsaxcompanions.com
Dynamics AX Companions
- 265 -
www.blindsquirrelpublishing.com
© 2015 Blind Squirrel Publishing, LLC , All Rights Reserved
 BLIND SQUIRREL
PUBLISHING

It is already defaulting focus to the Item Number field so all you need to do is type in part of the part code that you are searching for just like you did for the customer.

Then you have found the right product, just press the ENTER key to select it.

If you want to access a feature within the ribbon bar as you are entering in the order then you can use the Show Me option by clicking on the lightbulb icon, or by pressing ALT+Q.

Just type in the feature that you are looking for and you will see all of the matching options.

Then select the menu item that matches.

In this case we are looking at inventory availability and when we are done, just press ESC to exit out of the form.

After you have finished entering in the order details, just press ALT+S to save the record.

Then press ESC to exit from the form.

Now you are back to the Sales Order Processing and Inquiry form ready to do it over again.

Entering an order

How to do it…

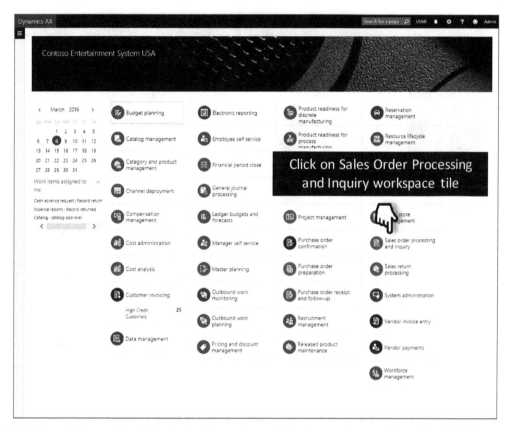

Start off by clicking on the Sales Order Processing and Inquiry workspace tile on the default dashboard.

da𝑥c www.dynamicsaxcompanions.com
Dynamics AX Companions
- 267 -
www.blindsquirrelpublishing.com
© 2015 Blind Squirrel Publishing, LLC , All Rights Reserved
BLIND SQUIRREL
PUBLISHING

Entering an order

How to do it...

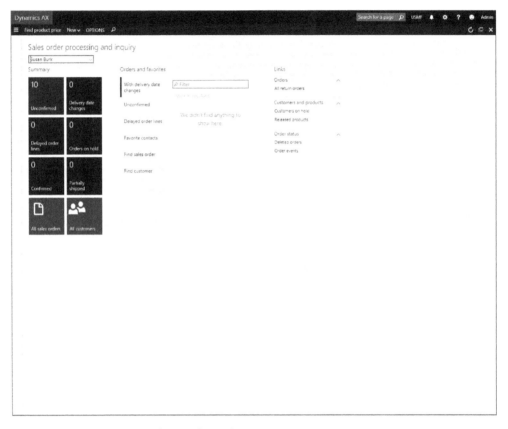

This will open up the main workspace for order entry.

Entering an order

How to do it...

Now press ALT+N to access the New menu item and then click the DOWN ARROW to see the menu items. From here you can select the Sales Order menu item.

daxc   www.dynamicsaxcompanions.com
Dynamics AX Companions
- 269 -
www.blindsquirrelpublishing.com
© 2015 Blind Squirrel Publishing, LLC , All Rights Reserved
BLIND SQUIRREL
PUBLISHING

Entering an order

How to do it…

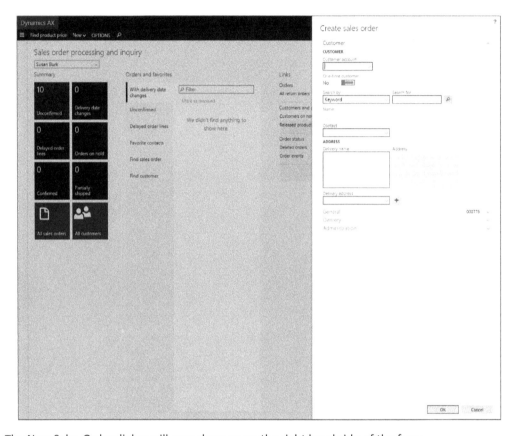

The New Sales Order dialog will now show up on the right hand side of the form.

Entering an order

How to do it…

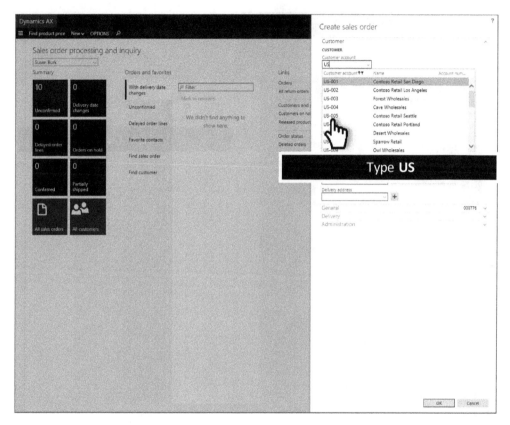

To select a customer, just type in part of the customer details that you want to search on. If you type in part of the account number then it will show you all of the account numbers that match using the search ahead feature.

da✕c www.dynamicsaxcompanions.com
Dynamics AX Companions

- 271 -

www.blindsquirrelpublishing.com
© 2015 Blind Squirrel Publishing, LLC , All Rights Reserved

BLIND SQUIRREL
PUBLISHING

Entering an order

How to do it…

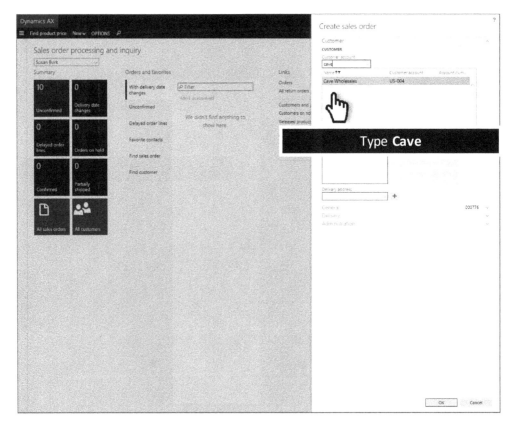

If you type in something that is found in some of the other columns – like the name for example then the system is smart enough to match it up to the other columns.

Entering an order

How to do it…

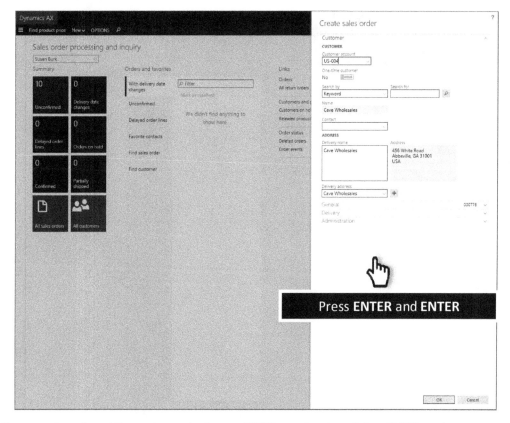

Once you have found the customer just press ENTER to select it and then ENTER again to create the new sales order.

daxc   www.dynamicsaxcompanions.com
Dynamics AX Companions
- 273 -
www.blindsquirrelpublishing.com
© 2015 Blind Squirrel Publishing, LLC , All Rights Reserved
BLIND SQUIRREL PUBLISHING

Entering an order

How to do it...

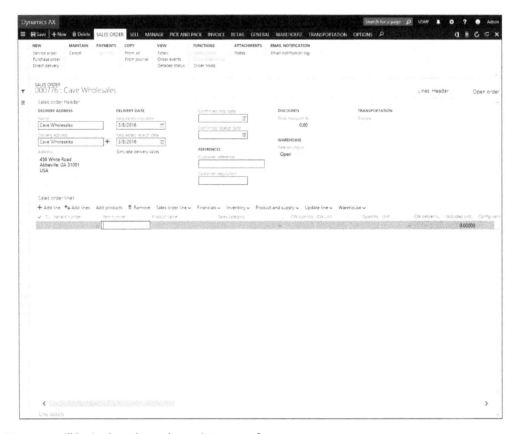

Now you will be in the sales order maintenance form.

daxc www.dynamicsaxcompanions.com
Dynamics AX Companions

- 274 -

www.blindsquirrelpublishing.com
© 2015 Blind Squirrel Publishing, LLC , All Rights Reserved

BLIND SQUIRREL
PUBLISHING

Entering an order

How to do it…

It is already defaulting focus to the Item Number field so all you need to do is type in part of the part code that you are searching for just like you did for the customer.

Entering an order

How to do it…

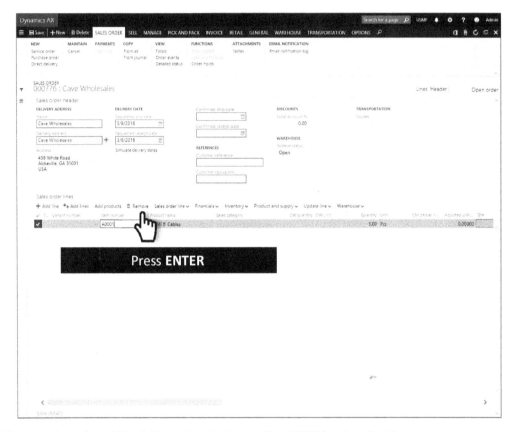

Then you have found the right product, just press the ENTER key to select it.

da✕c   www.dynamicsaxcompanions.com
Dynamics AX Companions

BLIND SQUIRREL
PUBLISHING

Entering an order

How to do it...

If you want to access a feature within the ribbon bar as you are entering in the order then you can use the Show Me option by clicking on the lightbulb icon, or by pressing ALT+Q.

da𝑥c   www.dynamicsaxcompanions.com
Dynamics AX Companions

- 277 -

www.blindsquirrelpublishing.com
© 2015 Blind Squirrel Publishing, LLC , All Rights Reserved

BLIND SQUIRREL
PUBLISHING

Entering an order

How to do it...

Just type in the feature that you are looking for and you will see all of the matching options.

Entering an order

How to do it…

Then select the menu item that matches.

Entering an order

How to do it…

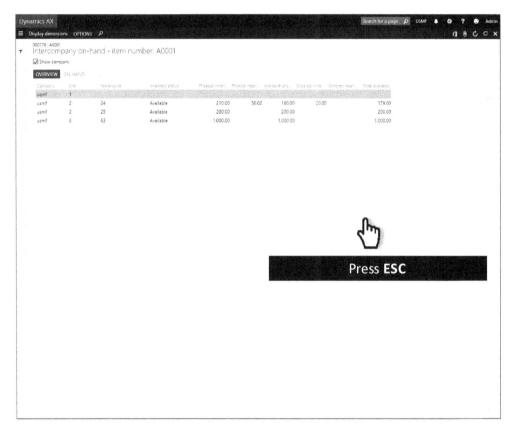

In this case we are looking at inventory availability and when we are done, just press ESC to exit out of the form.

daxc   www.dynamicsaxcompanions.com
Dynamics AX Companions

www.blindsquirrelpublishing.com
© 2015 Blind Squirrel Publishing, LLC , All Rights Reserved

BLIND SQUIRREL
PUBLISHING

Entering an order

How to do it…

After you have finished entering in the order details, just press ALT+S to save the record.

da⅔c   www.dynamicsaxcompanions.com
Dynamics AX Companions

- 281 -

www.blindsquirrelpublishing.com
© 2015 Blind Squirrel Publishing, LLC , All Rights Reserved

BLIND SQUIRREL
PUBLISHING

Entering an order

How to do it…

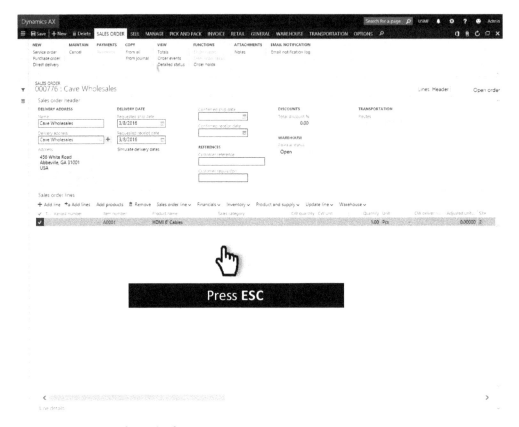

Then press ESC to exit from the form.

daxc www.dynamicsaxcompanions.com
Dynamics AX Companions
- 282 -
www.blindsquirrelpublishing.com
© 2015 Blind Squirrel Publishing, LLC , All Rights Reserved
BLIND SQUIRREL
PUBLISHING

Entering an order

How to do it...

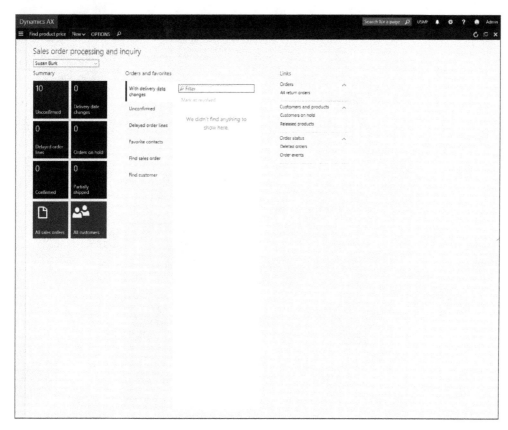

Now you are back to the Sales Order Processing and Inquiry form ready to do it over again.

Accessing the help

The new Dynamics AX has a lot of inbuilt context sensitive help that you can take advantage of, but these are not your common help options. Users are able to access context sensitive help directly from the application including Wiki curations and also the new interactive task guides.

How to do it...

To access the help, just click on the ? icon in the top right hand corner of the application.

This will open up the help panel showing you all of the task guides that are associated with the application. These are special types of help that will step you through the recorded tasks interactively click by click.

The new Dynamics AX also comes with a new type of help through a curated Wiki. This allows Microsoft, Partners, and Customers to contribute to the help for dynamics AX collaboratively. To access this, just click on the Wiki tab on the help panel.

Then the Wiki tab is shown if there is any help that is related to the screen that you are on then it will show here, and if not, then you will be able to search the Wiki help by just typing in the topic that you are interested in.

daℵc   www.dynamicsaxcompanions.com
Dynamics AX Companions

- 285 -

www.blindsquirrelpublishing.com
© 2015 Blind Squirrel Publishing, LLC , All Rights Reserved

 BLIND SQUIRREL
PUBLISHING

Accessing the help

How to do it…

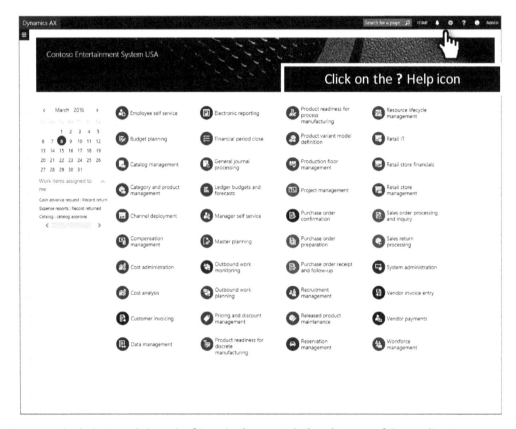

To access the help, just click on the ? icon in the top right hand corner of the application.

www.dynamicsaxcompanions.com
Dynamics AX Companions

- 286 -

www.blindsquirrelpublishing.com
© 2015 Blind Squirrel Publishing, LLC , All Rights Reserved

BLIND SQUIRREL
PUBLISHING

Accessing the help

How to do it...

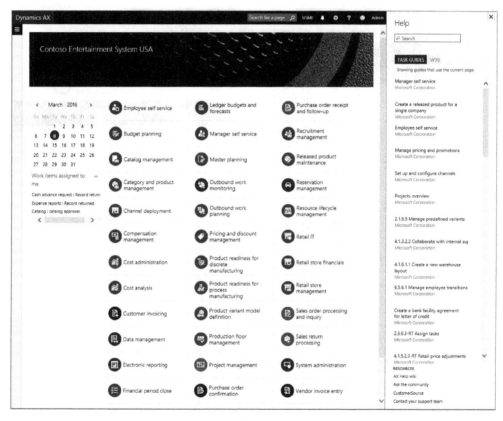

This will open up the help panel showing you all of the task guides that are associated with the application. These are special types of help that will step you through the recorded tasks interactively click by click.

daxc www.dynamicsaxcompanions.com
Dynamics AX Companions

- 287 -

www.blindsquirrelpublishing.com
© 2015 Blind Squirrel Publishing, LLC , All Rights Reserved

BLIND SQUIRREL
PUBLISHING

Accessing the help

How to do it…

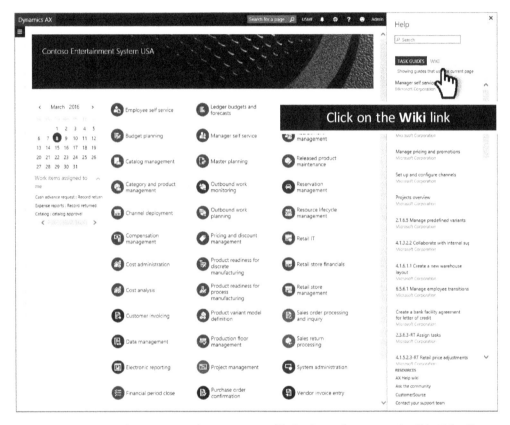

The new Dynamics AX also comes with a new type of help through a curated Wiki. This allows Microsoft, Partners, and Customers to contribute to the help for dynamics AX collaboratively. To access this, just click on the Wiki tab on the help panel.

daxc   www.dynamicsaxcompanions.com
Dynamics AX Companions
- 288 -
www.blindsquirrelpublishing.com
© 2015 Blind Squirrel Publishing, LLC , All Rights Reserved
BLIND SQUIRREL PUBLISHING

Accessing the help

How to do it...

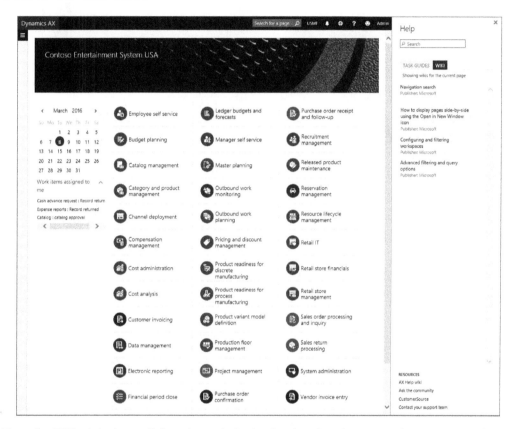

Then the Wiki tab is shown if there is any help that is related to the screen that you are on then it will show here, and if not, then you will be able to search the Wiki help by just typing in the topic that you are interested in.

Using the Wiki help

The Wiki help is a different generation of help that is being delivered with Dynamics AX. Rather than just having help that is delivered with the application and never updated, the Wiki help is a community curated help system where Microsoft, Partners and even customers are able to contribute and update the content.

How to do it...

To see the Wiki help in action, just click on the Sales Order Processing and Inquiry tile within the default dashboard.

Then click on the All Sales Order tile on the left hand side of the Sales order processing and inquiry workspace.

Then when the All sales orders list page is displayed, click on any of the orders.

You will notice that the Wiki help list refreshed because there are a number of help topics that are specifically associated with this form.

For example, you can click on the Credit card setup, authentication and capture link in the wiki help if you want more information about the credit card processing.

This will take you to the wiki help companion website with all of the information regarding credit card processing.

 www.dynamicsaxcompanions.com
Dynamics AX Companions

- 291 -

www.blindsquirrelpublishing.com
© 2015 Blind Squirrel Publishing, LLC , All Rights Reserved

 BLIND SQUIRREL
PUBLISHING

Using the Wiki help

How to do it…

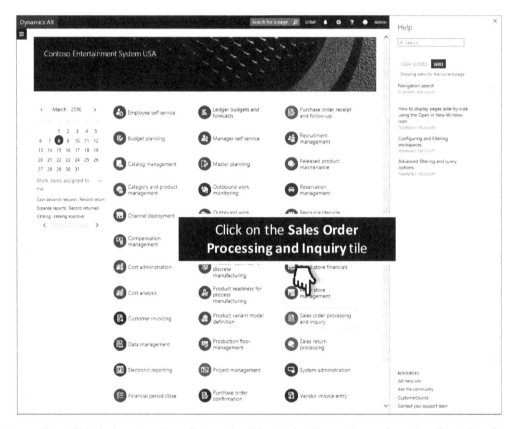

To see the Wiki help in action, just click on the Sales Order Processing and Inquiry tile within the default dashboard.

Using the Wiki help

How to do it…

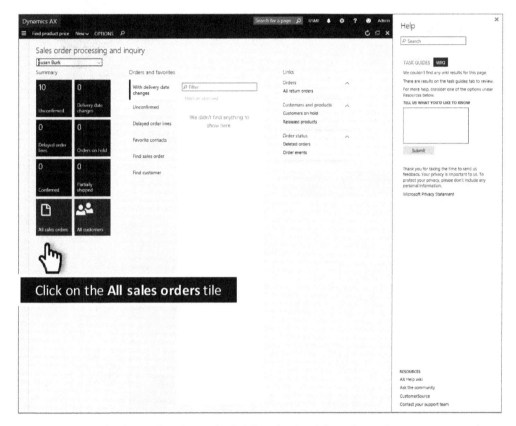

Click on the **All sales orders** tile

Then click on the All Sales Order tile on the left hand side of the Sales order processing and inquiry workspace.

daxc   www.dynamicsaxcompanions.com
Dynamics AX Companions
- 293 -
www.blindsquirrelpublishing.com
© 2015 Blind Squirrel Publishing, LLC , All Rights Reserved
BLIND SQUIRREL
PUBLISHING

Using the Wiki help

How to do it…

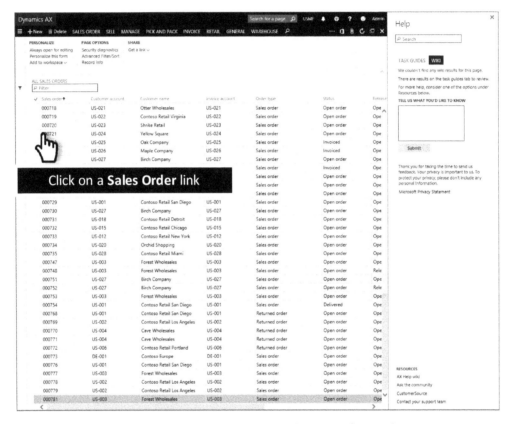

Then when the All sales orders list page is displayed, click on any of the orders.

Using the Wiki help

How to do it…

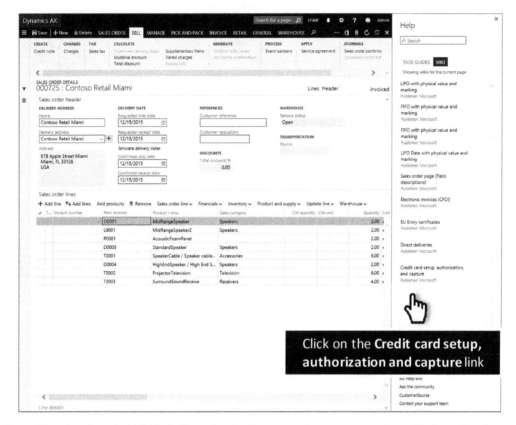

You will notice that the Wiki help list refreshed because there are a number of help topics that are specifically associated with this form.

For example, you can click on the Credit card setup, authentication and capture link in the wiki help if you want more information about the credit card processing.

daxc   www.dynamicsaxcompanions.com
       Dynamics AX Companions
       - 295 -
       www.blindsquirrelpublishing.com
       © 2015 Blind Squirrel Publishing, LLC , All Rights Reserved
       BLIND SQUIRREL
       PUBLISHING

Using the Wiki help

How to do it…

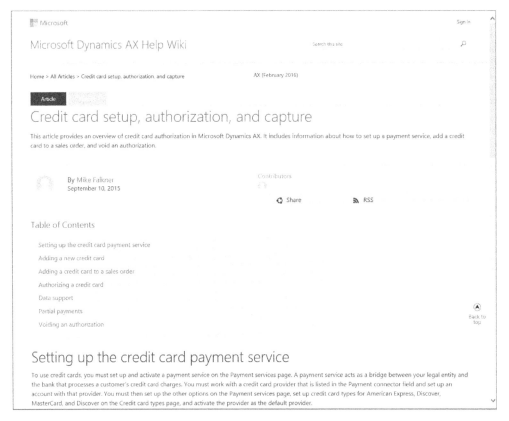

This will take you to the wiki help companion website with all of the information regarding credit card processing.

 www.dynamicsaxcompanions.com
Dynamics AX Companions
- 296 -
www.blindsquirrelpublishing.com
© 2015 Blind Squirrel Publishing, LLC , All Rights Reserved
BLIND SQUIRREL PUBLISHING

Using the task guides

If you ware looking for a more interactive type of help with the new Dynamics AX, or if you are looking to learn how to perform a certain task then you will probably want to use the Task Guides. These are great because they actually step you through steps required to perform a task within Dynamics AX.

How to do it...

To see all of the Task Guides that are related to the current form that you are in, just click on the Task Guides tab within the Help panel.

When the task guides refresh you will see that there are a lot of task guides that you can step through.

For example, if you want to learn how to create a new sales order then click on the Create Sales Order link in the task guides.

This will open up a new panel for the task guide that shows you the narrative steps that explain how you perform the task.

But if you want more help, just click on the Start Task Guide button at the bottom of the panel.

This will start stepping you through all of the steps interactively, and tell you what you need to click on.

For example, the first step is to open up the Shipped but not Invoiced Sales Orders from the dropdown menu.

After you have done this then you will be asked to click on the New button on the menu bar.

da×c   www.dynamicsaxcompanions.com
Dynamics AX Companions
   - 297 -
www.blindsquirrelpublishing.com
© 2015 Blind Squirrel Publishing, LLC , All Rights Reserved
 BLIND SQUIRREL
PUBLISHING

So you should click it.

Then click on the close button just like it tells you

You can continue through this process all of the way to the end if you like just by following the prompts.

Using the task guides

How to do it...

To see all of the Task Guides that are related to the current form that you are in, just click on the Task Guides tab within the Help panel.

www.dynamicsaxcompanions.com
Dynamics AX Companions
- 298 -
www.blindsquirrelpublishing.com
© 2015 Blind Squirrel Publishing, LLC , All Rights Reserved
BLIND SQUIRREL
PUBLISHING

Using the task guides

How to do it...

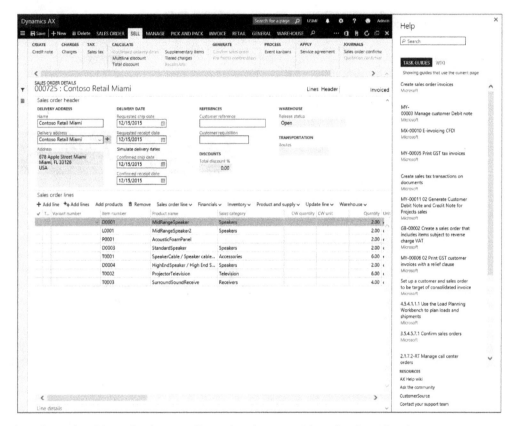

When the task guides refresh you will see that there are a lot of task guides that you can step through.

daxc   www.dynamicsaxcompanions.com
Dynamics AX Companions
- 299 -
www.blindsquirrelpublishing.com
© 2015 Blind Squirrel Publishing, LLC , All Rights Reserved
 BLIND SQUIRREL PUBLISHING

Using the task guides

How to do it…

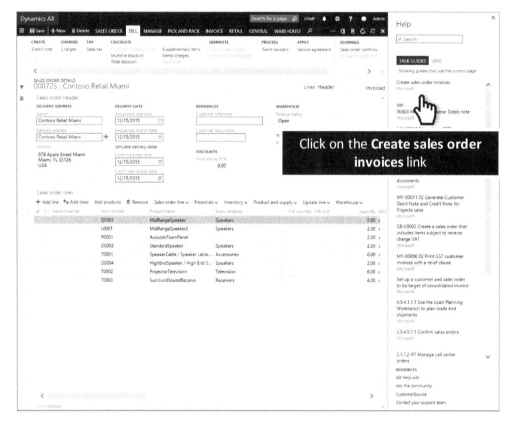

For example, if you want to learn how to create a new sales order then click on the Create Sales Order link in the task guides.

Using the task guides

How to do it…

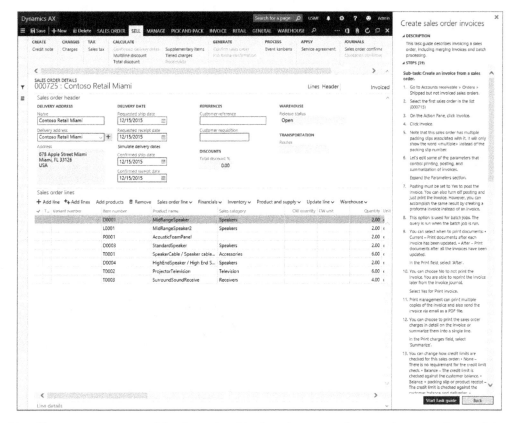

This will open up a new panel for the task guide that shows you the narrative steps that explain how you perform the task.

da⨯c   www.dynamicsaxcompanions.com
Dynamics AX Companions
- 301 -
www.blindsquirrelpublishing.com
© 2015 Blind Squirrel Publishing, LLC , All Rights Reserved
BLIND SQUIRREL PUBLISHING

Using the task guides

How to do it…

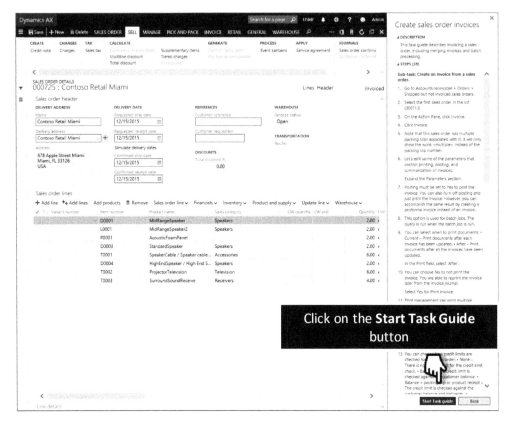

But if you want more help, just click on the Start Task Guide button at the bottom of the panel.

Using the task guides

How to do it...

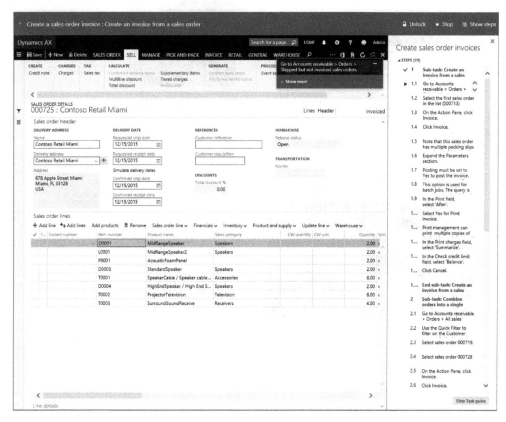

This will start stepping you through all of the steps interactively, and tell you what you need to click on.

www.blindsquirrelpublishing.com
© 2015 Blind Squirrel Publishing, LLC , All Rights Reserved

 BLIND SQUIRREL PUBLISHING

Using the task guides

How to do it…

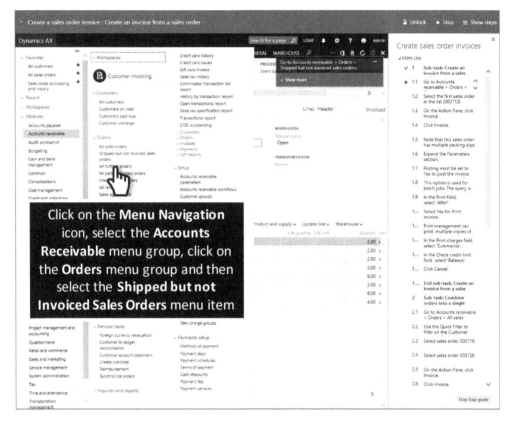

For example, the first step is to open up the Shipped but not Invoiced Sales Orders from the dropdown menu.

Using the task guides

How to do it...

After you have done this then you will be asked to click on the New button on the menu bar.

da&c   www.dynamicsaxcompanions.com
Dynamics AX Companions
- 305 -
www.blindsquirrelpublishing.com
© 2015 Blind Squirrel Publishing, LLC , All Rights Reserved
BLIND SQUIRREL PUBLISHING

Using the task guides

How to do it…

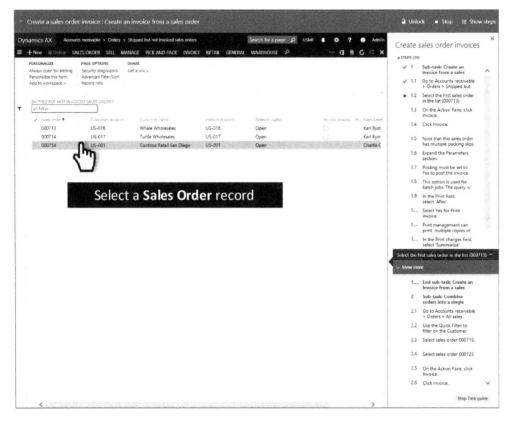

So you should click it.

Using the task guides

How to do it...

Then click on the close button just like it tells you

Using the task guides

How to do it…

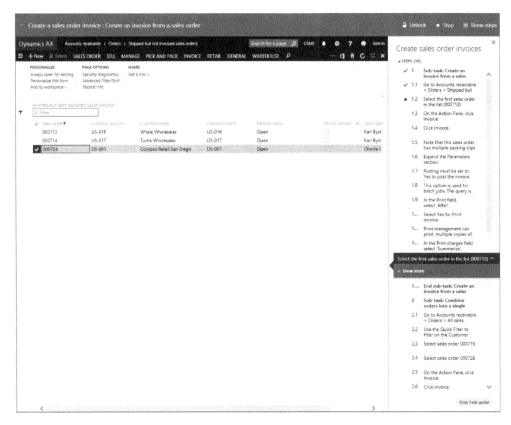

You can continue through this process all of the way to the end if you like just by following the prompts.

daxc
www.dynamicsaxcompanions.com
Dynamics AX Companions
- 308 -
www.blindsquirrelpublishing.com
© 2015 Blind Squirrel Publishing, LLC , All Rights Reserved
BLIND SQUIRREL
PUBLISHING

Creating your own task guides

There is one more special feature that is available with the Task Guides, and that is that you can create your own recordings that you can play back later on, just by performing the task yourself. This means that you can document your own business processes just like the standard ones delivered with the new Dynamics AX.

How to do it...

To do this, first click on the Gear icon in the top right hand corner of the application.

When the dropdown list is displayed, select the Task Recorder option.

This will open up the Task Recorder panel on the right hand side of the form.

To create a new recording, just click on the Create Recording link.

This will take you to the Task Recording creation form.

Just type in a Recording Name to describe the recording.

And then type in a Recording description to explain what you are doing within the recording.

When you have done that, click on the Start button at the bottom of the panel.

This will open up a recording bar at the top of the form showing you that you are in recording mode.

All you need to do is then step through the motions of the task. For example, click on the Menu Navigation icon, select the Accounts Receivable menu group, click on the Orders menu group and then select the All Sales Orders menu item

Then click on the New button in the menu bar.

Notice on the right hand side of the form, each of the steps that we are walking through is being recorded and tracked within the Task recording.

Now just type in a Customer account and press enter.

This will take you to the order lines form.

Now type in an Item Number.

And also a Quantity.

And finish off by entering in a Site and Warehouse if you need to.

When you are done, and want to save the recording, just click on the Stop button in the recording controls bar.

Now you have recorded your task.

Creating your own task guides

How to do it…

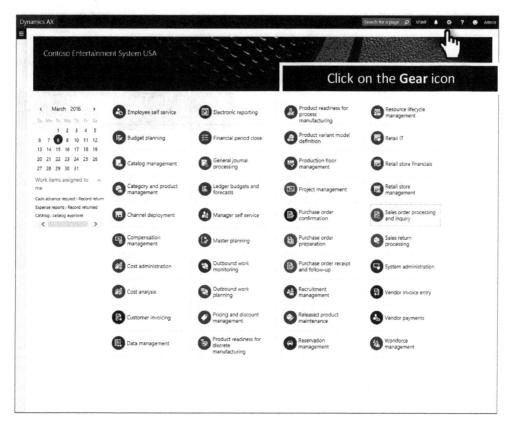

To do this, first click on the Gear icon in the top right hand corner of the application.

Creating your own task guides

How to do it…

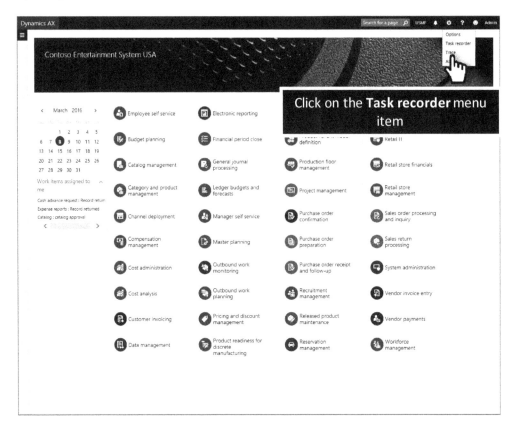

When the dropdown list is displayed, select the Task Recorder option.

Creating your own task guides

How to do it…

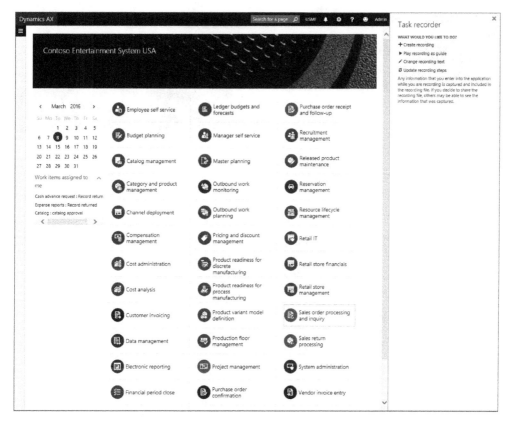

This will open up the Task Recorder panel on the right hand side of the form.

Creating your own task guides

How to do it…

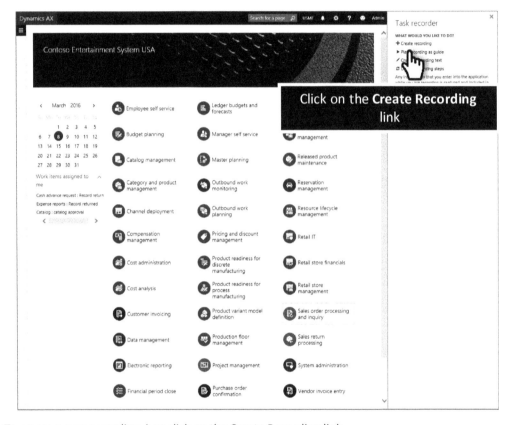

To create a new recording, just click on the Create Recording link.

Creating your own task guides

How to do it…

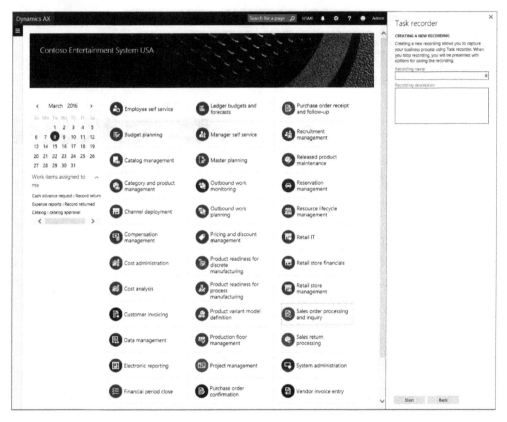

This will take you to the Task Recording creation form.

daxc   www.dynamicsaxcompanions.com
Dynamics AX Companions

www.blindsquirrelpublishing.com
© 2015 Blind Squirrel Publishing, LLC , All Rights Reserved

BLIND SQUIRREL
PUBLISHING

Creating your own task guides

How to do it…

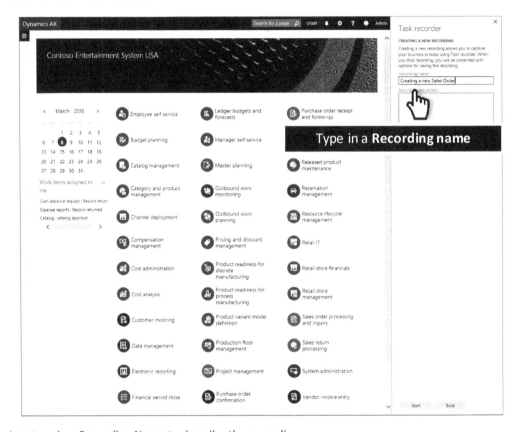

Just type in a Recording Name to describe the recording.

Creating your own task guides

How to do it…

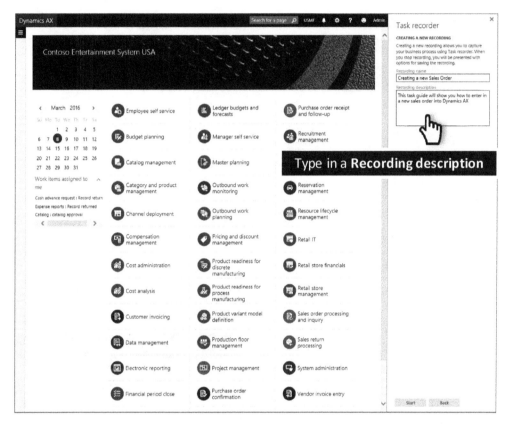

And then type in a Recording description to explain what you are doing within the recording.

daxc
www.dynamicsaxcompanions.com
Dynamics AX Companions

- 317 -

www.blindsquirrelpublishing.com
© 2015 Blind Squirrel Publishing, LLC , All Rights Reserved
BLIND SQUIRREL PUBLISHING

Creating your own task guides

How to do it…

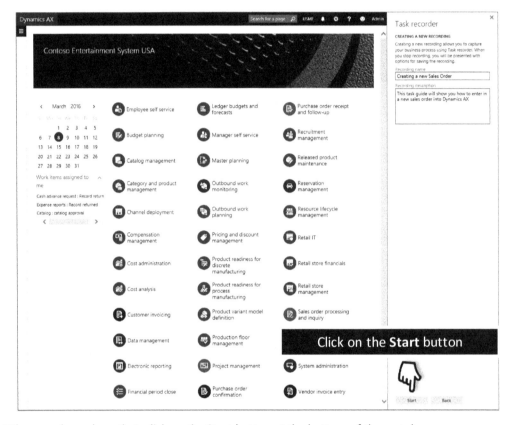

When you have done that, click on the Start button at the bottom of the panel.

Creating your own task guides

How to do it...

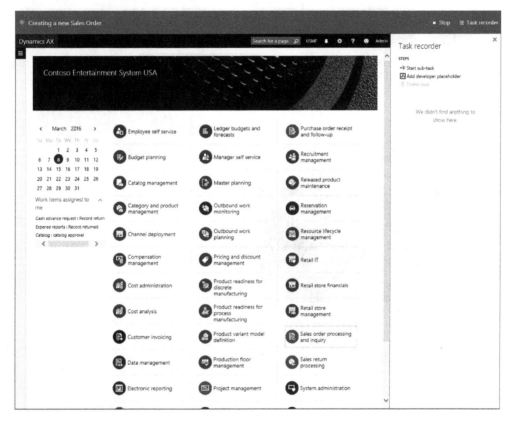

This will open up a recording bar at the top of the form showing you that you are in recording mode.

daxc
www.dynamicsaxcompanions.com
Dynamics AX Companions

www.blindsquirrelpublishing.com
© 2015 Blind Squirrel Publishing, LLC , All Rights Reserved

BLIND SQUIRREL
PUBLISHING

Creating your own task guides

How to do it…

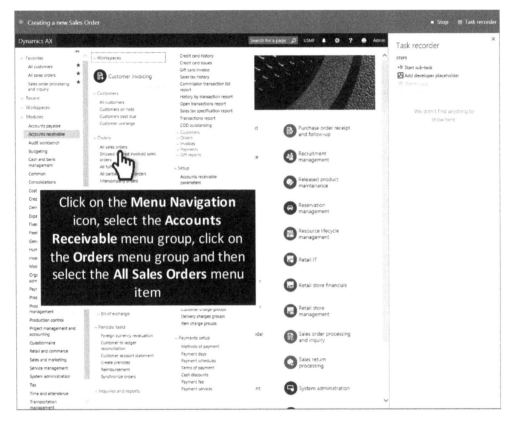

All you need to do is then step through the motions of the task. For example, click on the Menu Navigation icon, select the Accounts Receivable menu group, click on the Orders menu group and then select the All Sales Orders menu item

da⅂c   www.dynamicsaxcompanions.com
Dynamics AX Companions

- 320 -

www.blindsquirrelpublishing.com
© 2015 Blind Squirrel Publishing, LLC , All Rights Reserved

BLIND SQUIRREL
PUBLISHING

Creating your own task guides

How to do it…

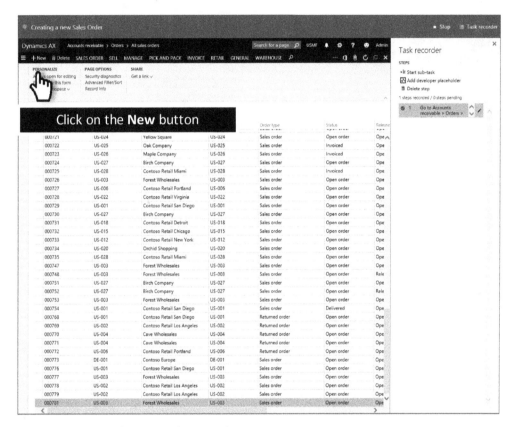

Then click on the New button in the menu bar.

da×c   www.dynamicsaxcompanions.com
Dynamics AX Companions

www.blindsquirrelpublishing.com
© 2015 Blind Squirrel Publishing, LLC , All Rights Reserved

BLIND SQUIRREL
PUBLISHING

Creating your own task guides

How to do it…

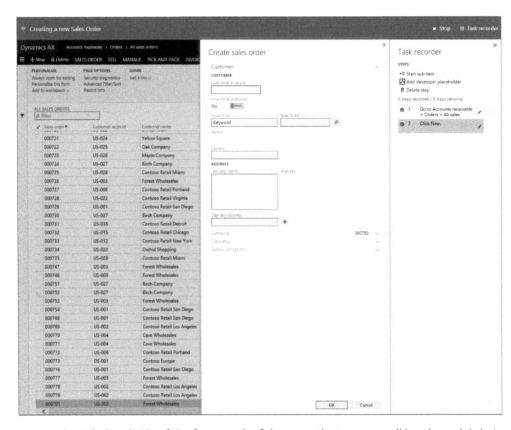

Notice on the right hand side of the form, each of the steps that we are walking through is being recorded and tracked within the Task recording.

Creating your own task guides

How to do it...

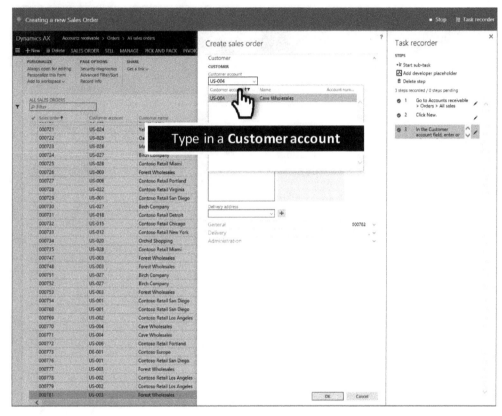

Now just type in a Customer account and press enter.

daxc www.dynamicsaxcompanions.com
Dynamics AX Companions
- 323 -
www.blindsquirrelpublishing.com
© 2015 Blind Squirrel Publishing, LLC , All Rights Reserved
BLIND SQUIRREL
PUBLISHING

Creating your own task guides

How to do it…

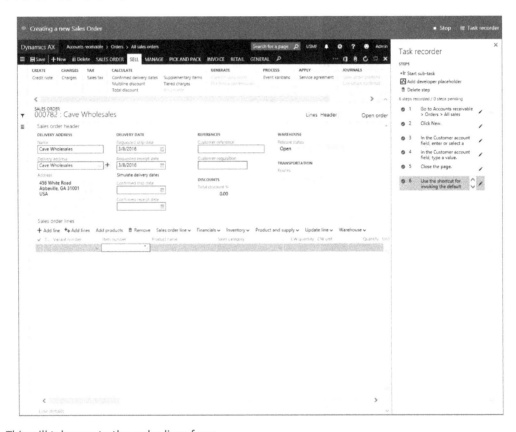

This will take you to the order lines form.

Creating your own task guides

How to do it…

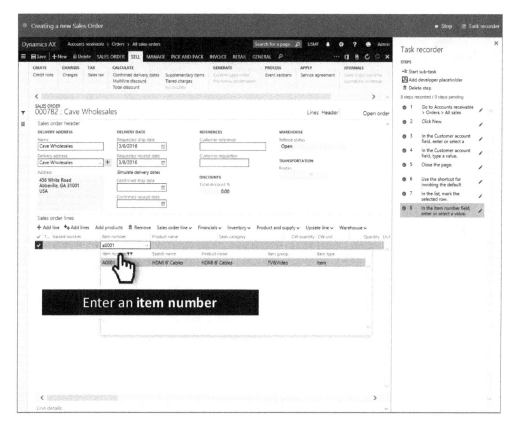

Now type in an Item Number.

www.dynamicsaxcompanions.com
Dynamics AX Companions
www.blindsquirrelpublishing.com
© 2015 Blind Squirrel Publishing, LLC , All Rights Reserved
BLIND SQUIRREL PUBLISHING

Creating your own task guides

How to do it...

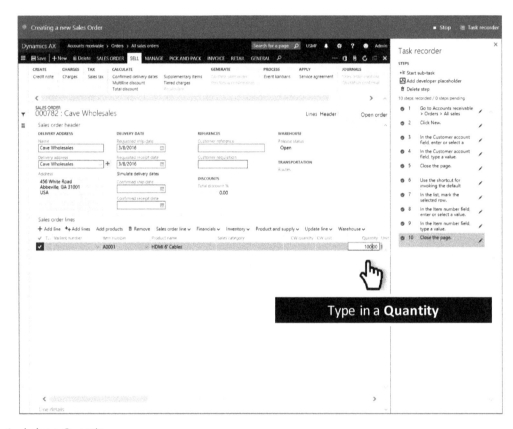

And also a Quantity.

Creating your own task guides

How to do it...

And finish off by entering in a Site and Warehouse if you need to.

When you are done, and want to save the recording, just click on the Stop button in the recording controls bar.

Creating your own task guides

How to do it…

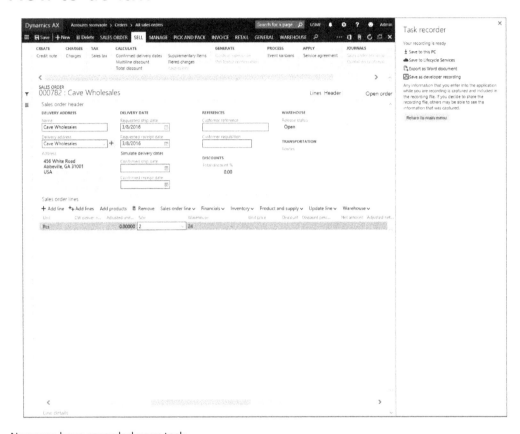

Now you have recorded your task.

Exporting task recordings to Lifecycle Services

Once you have created a task recording, you will want to store it somewhere so that everyone else is able to access it and use it while they are trying to learn the system. The best place to do this is within Lifecycle Services.

How to do it...

To saved the task recording in Lifecycle Services, just click on the Save to LCS link in the Task Recorder panel.

This will then connect to the default Lifecycle Services business proves model and show you all of the business process model categories as a tree structure.

All you need to do is expand out the business process models and find the node that matches the process that you just recorded.

After you have selected it then click on the OK button to save the task recording to Lifecycle Services.

And you are now done.

daxc www.dynamicsaxcompanions.com
Dynamics AX Companions
- 329 -
www.blindsquirrelpublishing.com
© 2015 Blind Squirrel Publishing, LLC , All Rights Reserved
 BLIND SQUIRREL
PUBLISHING

Exporting task recordings to Lifecycle Services

How to do it…

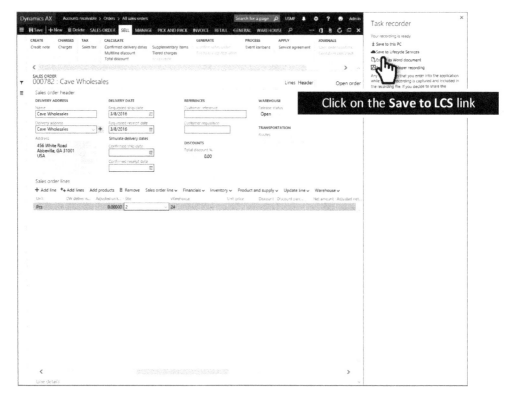

To saved the task recording in Lifecycle Services, just click on the Save to LCS link in the Task Recorder panel.

daxc www.dynamicsaxcompanions.com
Dynamics AX Companions
- 330 -
www.blindsquirrelpublishing.com
© 2015 Blind Squirrel Publishing, LLC , All Rights Reserved
 BLIND SQUIRREL PUBLISHING

Exporting task recordings to Lifecycle Services

How to do it...

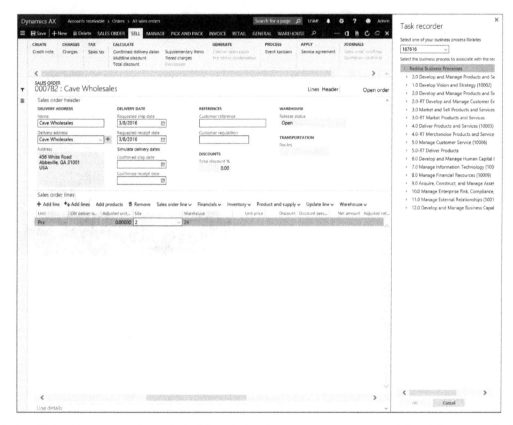

This will then connect to the default Lifecycle Services business proves model and show you all of the business process model categories as a tree structure.

Exporting task recordings to Lifecycle Services

How to do it…

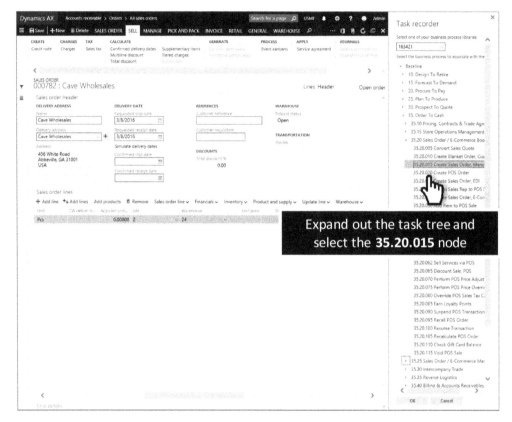

All you need to do is expand out the business process models and find the node that matches the process that you just recorded.

Exporting task recordings to Lifecycle Services

How to do it…

After you have selected it then click on the OK button to save the task recording to Lifecycle Services.

Exporting task recordings to Lifecycle Services

How to do it…

And you are now done.

Viewing task recordings in Lifecycle Services

All of the task recordings that you make are available within Lifecycle services, and you can see them when you browse the business process models.

How to do it...

The first step is to open up Lifecycle Services. There is a shortcut that you can use to get there. Start off by clicking on the System Administration workspace tile.

And then when the System Administration workspace is displayed, click on the Lifecycle Services tile.

This will take you into Lifecycle Services and you can then access the project that was created for your instance of Dynamics AX.

If you scroll over to the right and you will be able to click on the Business Process Modeler tile.

When you open up the Business Process Libraries select the library that you saved your task recording to.

da✗c www.dynamicsaxcompanions.com
Dynamics AX Companions
- 335 -
www.blindsquirrelpublishing.com
© 2015 Blind Squirrel Publishing, LLC , All Rights Reserved
 BLIND SQUIRREL
PUBLISHING

Within the Business Process Library you will see the same hierarchy that you saw when you were saving your task recordings to Lifecycle Services. If you expand out the process tree then you will be able to see that there is a task recording business process library now attached to the node.

To view the business process flow diagram, just click on the process flow icon.

That will take you to the definition of your task recording and also the swim name business process view showing all of the forms that are impacted by the business process.

Viewing task recordings in Lifecycle Services

How to do it…

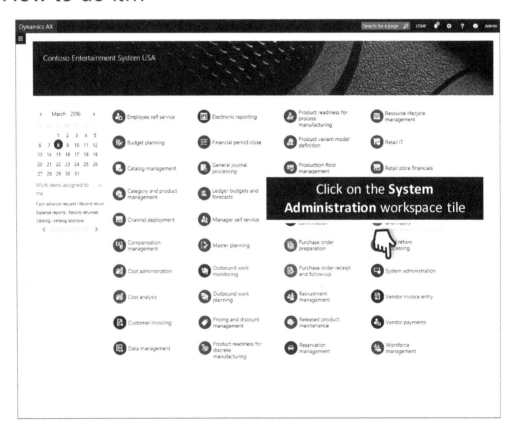

dayc www.dynamicsaxcompanions.com
Dynamics AX Companions
- 336 -
www.blindsquirrelpublishing.com
© 2015 Blind Squirrel Publishing, LLC , All Rights Reserved
BLIND SQUIRREL PUBLISHING

The first step is to open up Lifecycle Services. There is a shortcut that you can use to get there.
Start off by clicking on the System Administration workspace tile.

Viewing task recordings in Lifecycle Services

How to do it...

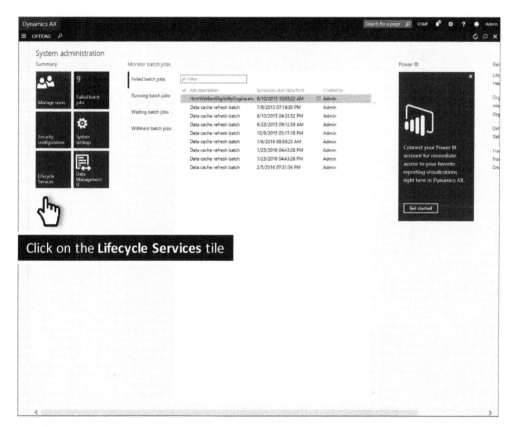

And then when the System Administration workspace is displayed, click on the Lifecycle Services
tile.

Viewing task recordings in Lifecycle Services

How to do it…

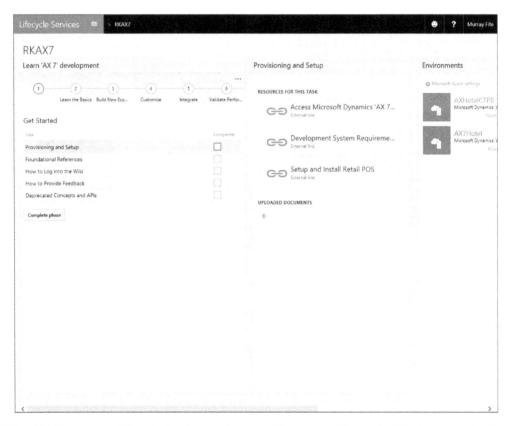

This will take you into Lifecycle Services and you can then access the project that was created for your instance of Dynamics AX.

daxc   www.dynamicsaxcompanions.com
       Dynamics AX Companions

- 338 -

www.blindsquirrelpublishing.com
© 2015 Blind Squirrel Publishing, LLC , All Rights Reserved

BLIND SQUIRREL
PUBLISHING

Viewing task recordings in Lifecycle Services

How to do it…

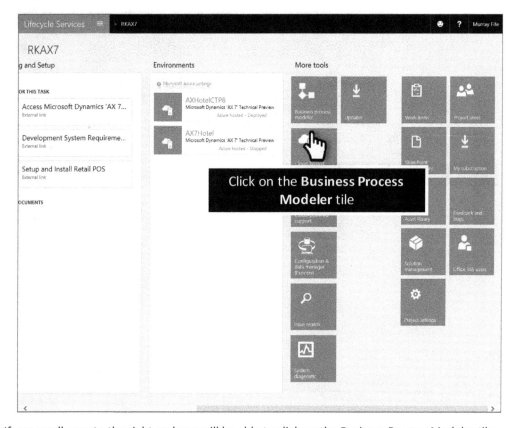

If you scroll over to the right and you will be able to click on the Business Process Modeler tile.

daxc www.dynamicsaxcompanions.com
Dynamics AX Companions
- 339 -
www.blindsquirrelpublishing.com
© 2015 Blind Squirrel Publishing, LLC , All Rights Reserved
BLIND SQUIRREL
PUBLISHING

Viewing task recordings in Lifecycle Services

How to do it…

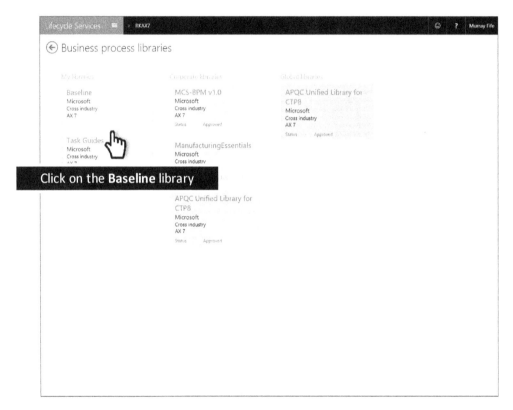

When you open up the Business Process Libraries select the library that you saved your task recording to.

daxc www.dynamicsaxcompanions.com
Dynamics AX Companions

- 340 -

www.blindsquirrelpublishing.com
© 2015 Blind Squirrel Publishing, LLC, All Rights Reserved

 BLIND SQUIRREL
PUBLISHING

Viewing task recordings in Lifecycle Services

How to do it…

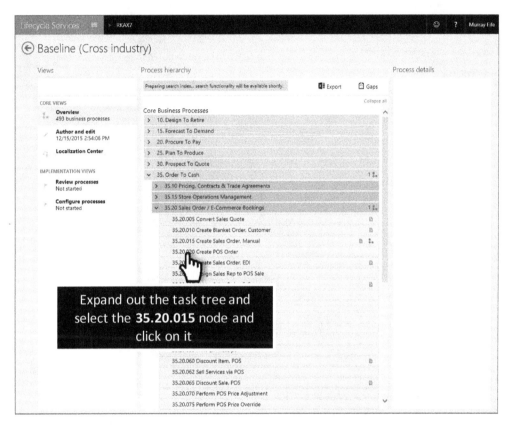

Within the Business Process Library you will see the same hierarchy that you saw when you were saving your task recordings to Lifecycle Services. If you expand out the process tree then you will be able to see that there is a task recording business process library now attached to the node.

daxc   www.dynamicsaxcompanions.com
Dynamics AX Companions
- 341 -
www.blindsquirrelpublishing.com
© 2015 Blind Squirrel Publishing, LLC , All Rights Reserved
BLIND SQUIRREL PUBLISHING

Viewing task recordings in Lifecycle Services

How to do it...

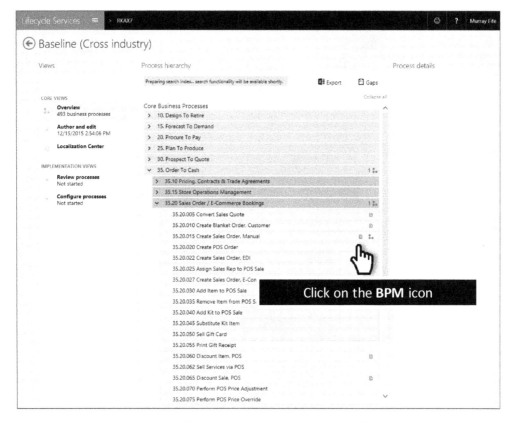

To view the business process flow diagram, just click on the process flow icon.

- 342 -

Viewing task recordings in Lifecycle Services

How to do it…

That will take you to the definition of your task recording and also the swim name business process view showing all of the forms that are impacted by the business process.

daxc   www.dynamicsaxcompanions.com
Dynamics AX Companions   - 343 -

www.blindsquirrelpublishing.com
© 2015 Blind Squirrel Publishing, LLC , All Rights Reserved

BLIND SQUIRREL
PUBLISHING

Changing the default company banner image

The personalization's that you can perform with the new Dynamics AX are not limited to just the user options. One of the new features is the ability to customize the default banner that shows up within the Default dashboard, and have a different banner by legal entity. This is a great way to add some branding to the application, and also a great way to allow you to see which company you are logging in to.

How to do it...

You do this through the Legal Entity maintenance within Dynamics AX. A quick way to find this form is to press CTRL+G to jump to the search bar within the header.

Then type in Legal and you will see all of the forms that match that search. In this case there is only one so you can then just click on it.

When the Legal Entities form is displayed, click on the Images fast tab to expand out the details.

Before we upload any new banners we need to make one quick change and that is to tell the system what it should be displaying on the company banner. To do this, click on the Dashboard company image type dropdown list.

Then select the Banner option to tell the system that we will be using a custom banner.

BLIND SQUIRREL PUBLISHING

You will notice that there is a new option here for the Dashboard Image. To change the image then click on the Change link.

You will notice that there is a new option here for the Dashboard Image. To change the image then click on the Change link.

This will open up a dialog panel where you can click on the Browse button.

This will open up a dialog box where you can search for the new banner image and then click on the Open button to select it.

When you return back to the Legal Entities form you will see that the image has been updated and all you need to do is click on the Save button.

When you return to the default workspace and press F5 to refresh the view then you will see that the banner has changed.

daxc   www.dynamicsaxcompanions.com
        Dynamics AX Companions

- 346 -

www.blindsquirrelpublishing.com
© 2015 Blind Squirrel Publishing, LLC , All Rights Reserved

BLIND SQUIRREL
PUBLISHING

Changing the default company banner image

How to do it…

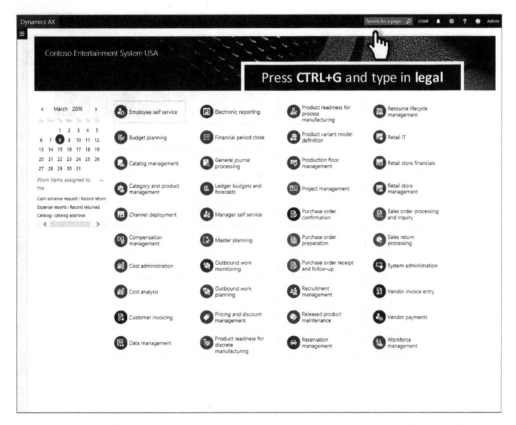

You do this through the Legal Entity maintenance within Dynamics AX. A quick way to find this form is to press CTRL+G to jump to the search bar within the header.

Changing the default company banner image

How to do it...

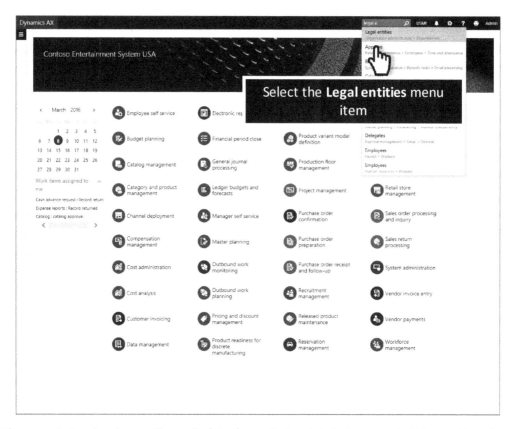

Then type in Legal and you will see all of the forms that match that search. In this case there is only one so you can then just click on it.

daxc www.dynamicsaxcompanions.com
Dynamics AX Companions
- 348 -
www.blindsquirrelpublishing.com
© 2015 Blind Squirrel Publishing, LLC , All Rights Reserved

BLIND SQUIRREL PUBLISHING

Changing the default company banner image

How to do it…

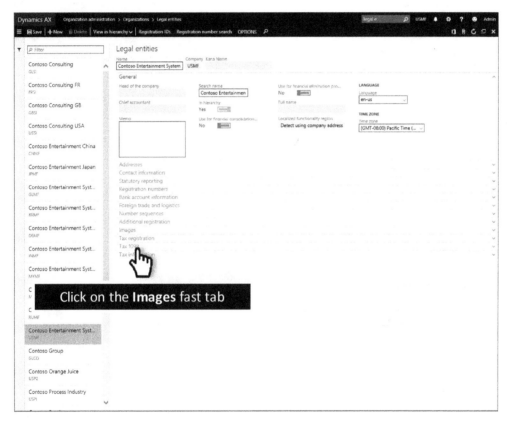

When the Legal Entities form is displayed, click on the Images fast tab to expand out the details.

dac www.dynamicsaxcompanions.com
Dynamics AX Companions

www.blindsquirrelpublishing.com
© 2015 Blind Squirrel Publishing, LLC , All Rights Reserved

BLIND SQUIRREL
PUBLISHING

Changing the default company banner image

How to do it…

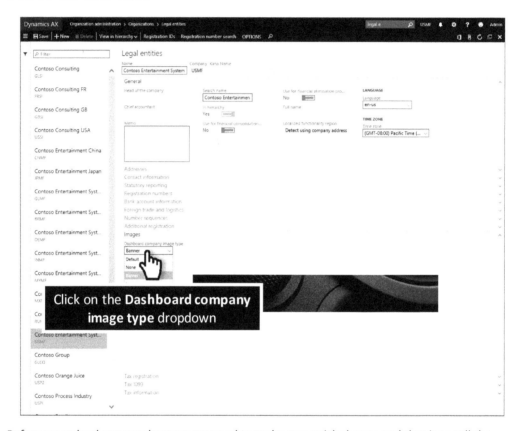

Click on the **Dashboard company image type** dropdown

Before we upload any new banners we need to make one quick change and that is to tell the system what it should be displaying on the company banner. To do this, click on the Dashboard company image type dropdown list.

da&c www.dynamicsaxcompanions.com
Dynamics AX Companions

- 350 -

www.blindsquirrelpublishing.com
© 2015 Blind Squirrel Publishing, LLC , All Rights Reserved

 BLIND SQUIRREL PUBLISHING

Changing the default company banner image

How to do it...

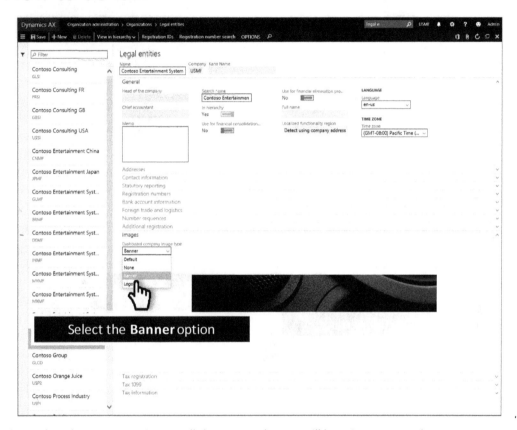

Then select the Banner option to tell the system that we will be using a custom banner.

Changing the default company banner image

How to do it…

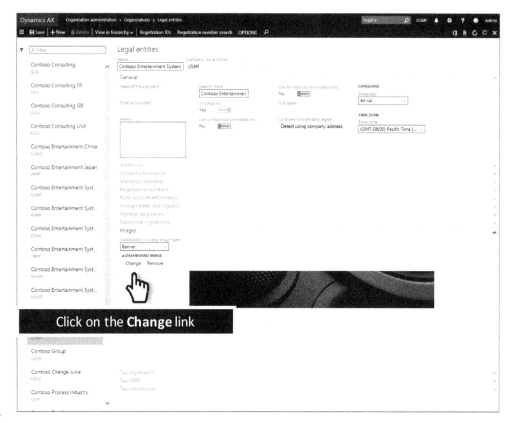

You will notice that there is a new option here for the Dashboard Image. To change the image then click on the Change link.

daxc   www.dynamicsaxcompanions.com
Dynamics AX Companions
- 352 -
www.blindsquirrelpublishing.com
© 2015 Blind Squirrel Publishing, LLC , All Rights Reserved

BLIND SQUIRREL PUBLISHING

Changing the default company banner image

How to do it...

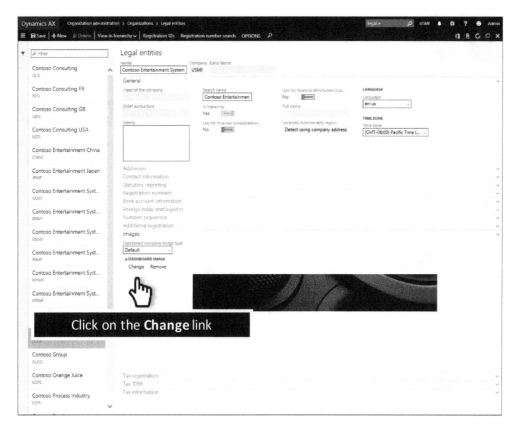

You will notice that there is a new option here for the Dashboard Image. To change the image then click on the Change link.

Changing the default company banner image

How to do it...

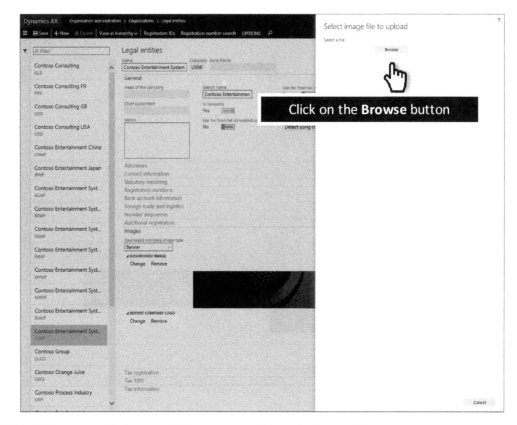

This will open up a dialog panel where you can click on the Browse button.

Changing the default company banner image

How to do it…

Select the new banner file and click on the **Open** button

This will open up a dialog box where you can search for the new banner image and then click on the Open button to select it.

dɑ✕c   www.dynamicsaxcompanions.com
Dynamics AX Companions

- 355 -

www.blindsquirrelpublishing.com
© 2015 Blind Squirrel Publishing, LLC , All Rights Reserved

BLIND SQUIRREL
PUBLISHING

Changing the default company banner image

How to do it…

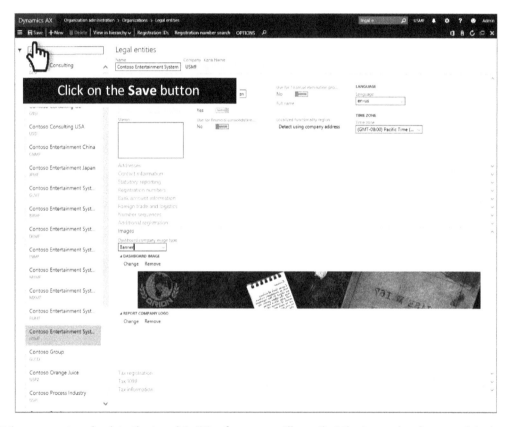

When you return back to the Legal Entities form you will see that the image has been updated and all you need to do is click on the Save button.

daxc   www.dynamicsaxcompanions.com
Dynamics AX Companions
- 356 -
www.blindsquirrelpublishing.com
© 2015 Blind Squirrel Publishing, LLC , All Rights Reserved
 BLIND SQUIRREL PUBLISHING

Changing the default company banner image

How to do it…

When you return to the default workspace and press F5 to refresh the view then you will see that the banner has changed.

Running financial reports

With the new Dynamics AX, the financial reporting is natively integrated within the application itself rather than being another separate reporting tool.

How to do it...

In order to access the Financial reports, start off by clicking on the Navigation menu to open up the menu navigation dropdown list.

Then click on the General Ledger menu group.

And then click on the Financial Reports menu item.

This will open up the Financial Reports list.

To run a report, all you need to do is click on the report name.

When the report is displayed, it is shown within the application itself.

If you want to drill into any of the detail then you just click on the currency value. For example you can click on the Cost of Goods Sold amount.

This will drill you down into the details for that made up the report line.

If you click on any of the other details then you will also get the option to drill further into the details.

To view the transactions within Dynamics AX, just click on the Open Account Transactions option.

That will take you straight to the transaction details within Dynamics AX where you can also browse to the original transactions..

Running financial reports

How to do it…

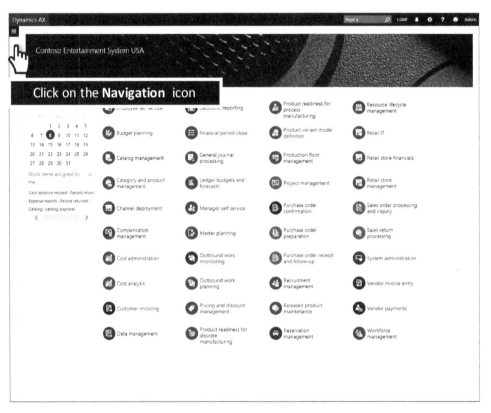

In order to access the Financial reports, start off by clicking on the Navigation menu to open up the menu navigation dropdown list.

Running financial reports

How to do it…

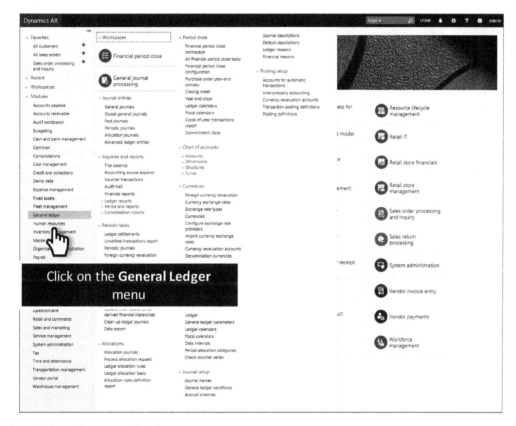

Then click on the General Ledger menu group.

Running financial reports

How to do it...

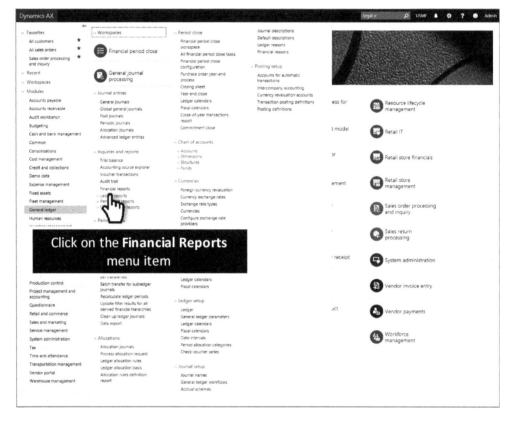

And then click on the Financial Reports menu item.

dac   www.dynamicsaxcompanions.com
Dynamics AX Companions
- 362 -
www.blindsquirrelpublishing.com
© 2015 Blind Squirrel Publishing, LLC , All Rights Reserved
BLIND SQUIRREL PUBLISHING

Running financial reports

How to do it...

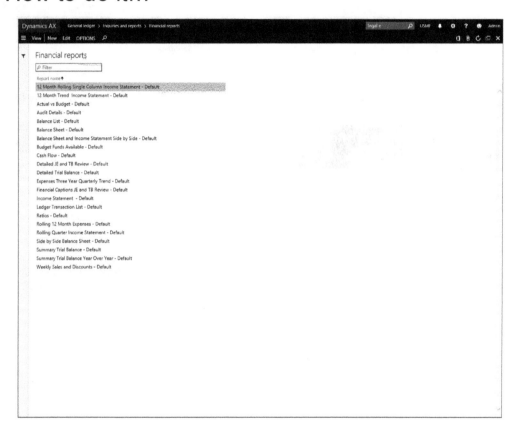

This will open up the Financial Reports list.

daxc   www.dynamicsaxcompanions.com
Dynamics AX Companions

www.blindsquirrelpublishing.com
© 2015 Blind Squirrel Publishing, LLC , All Rights Reserved

 BLIND SQUIRREL
PUBLISHING

Running financial reports

How to do it...

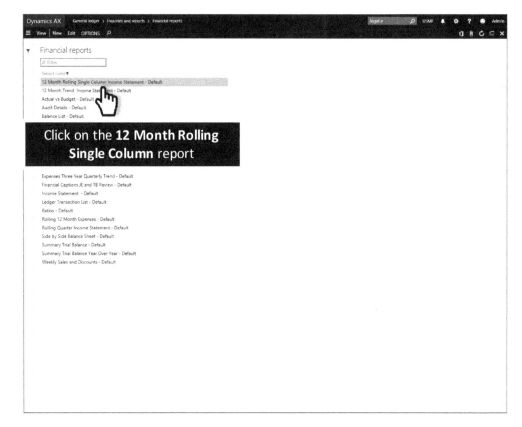

To run a report, all you need to do is click on the report name.

Running financial reports

How to do it…

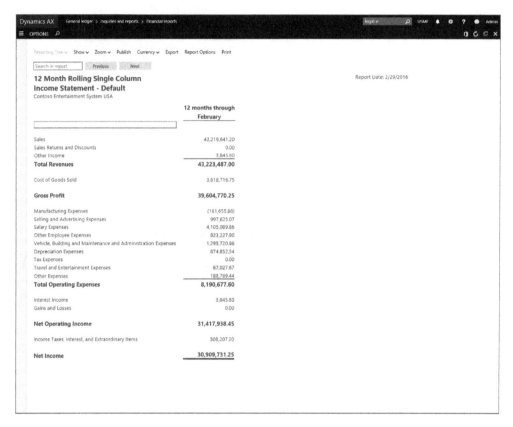

When the report is displayed, it is shown within the application itself.

daxc   www.dynamicsaxcompanions.com
Dynamics AX Companions

www.blindsquirrelpublishing.com
© 2015 Blind Squirrel Publishing, LLC , All Rights Reserved

BLIND SQUIRREL
PUBLISHING

Running financial reports

How to do it…

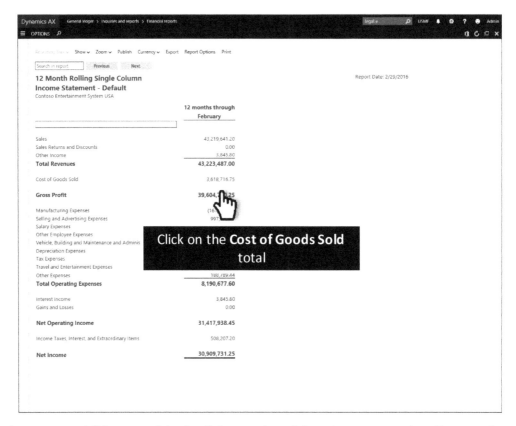

If you want to drill into any of the detail then you just click on the currency value. For example you can click on the Cost of Goods Sold amount.

Running financial reports

How to do it…

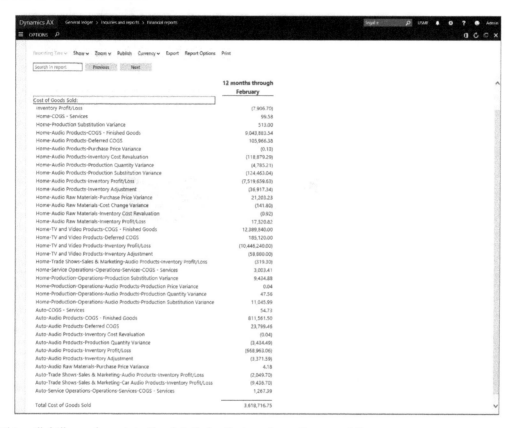

This will drill you down into the details for that made up the report line.

Running financial reports

How to do it…

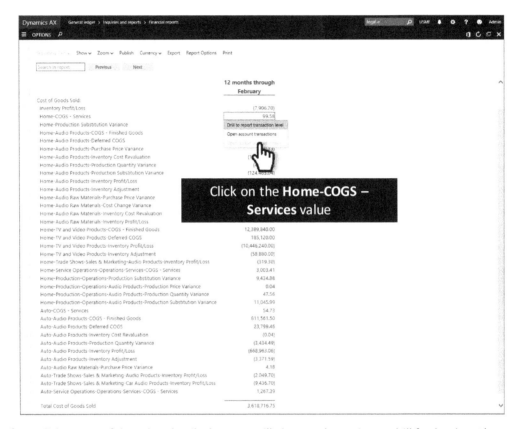

If you click on any of the other details then you will also get the option to drill further into the details.

Running financial reports

How to do it…

To view the transactions within Dynamics AX, just click on the Open Account Transactions option.

Running financial reports

How to do it…

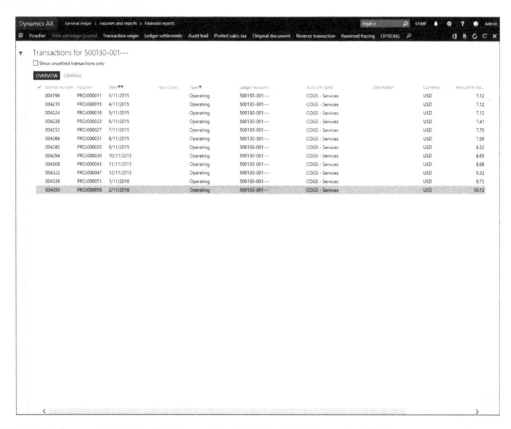

That will take you straight to the transaction details within Dynamics AX where you can also browse to the original transactions..

da✕c   www.dynamicsaxcompanions.com
Dynamics AX Companions

- 370 -

www.blindsquirrelpublishing.com
© 2015 Blind Squirrel Publishing, LLC , All Rights Reserved

BLIND SQUIRREL
PUBLISHING

Creating demo data

If you are working within a demo environment and you want to quickly hydrate the system with some demo data rather than typing it all in by hand so that features like the tiles show quantities and that there are detailed transactions for you to drill into then you can take advantage of the Demo Data build feature.

How to do it...

To do this, click on the Navigation menu icon in the header.

Then click on the Demo Data menu group.

And then click on the Generate data menu item.

This will open up a dialog panel that shows you all of the different workspaces that you can create the demo data.

Just enable any of the workspaces that you want to create the data for.

And then click on the OK button to start the demo data creation process.

The application will then start processing for a while as it creates your demo data.

It will may also give you some more feedback as it builds additional demo data such as the Financial Period Close data.

Now when you return to the workspaces you will see that there is demo data associated with the workspaces.

Creating demo data

How to do it…

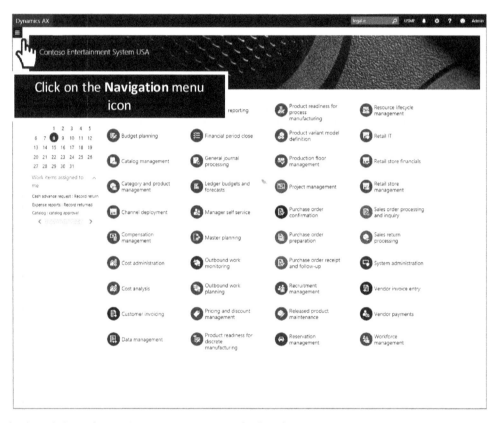

To do this, click on the Navigation menu icon in the header.

Creating demo data

How to do it…

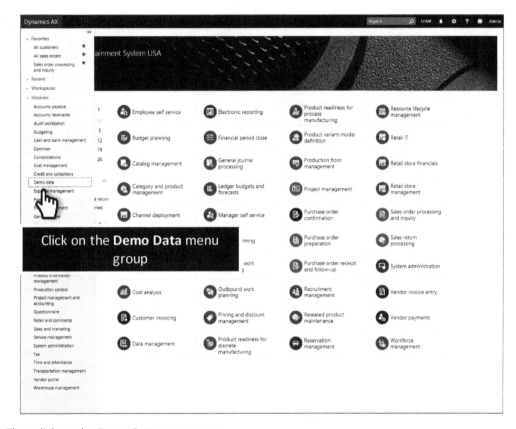

Then click on the Demo Data menu group.

Creating demo data

How to do it…

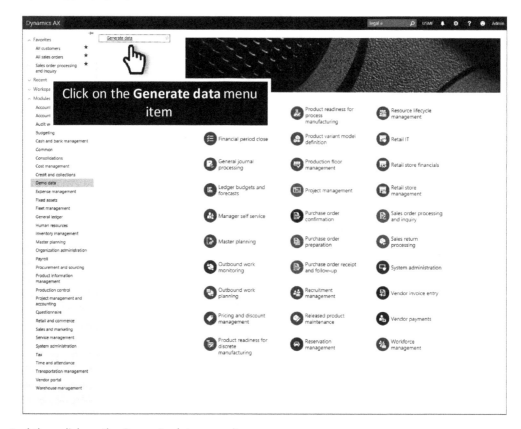

And then click on the Generate data menu item.

Creating demo data

How to do it…

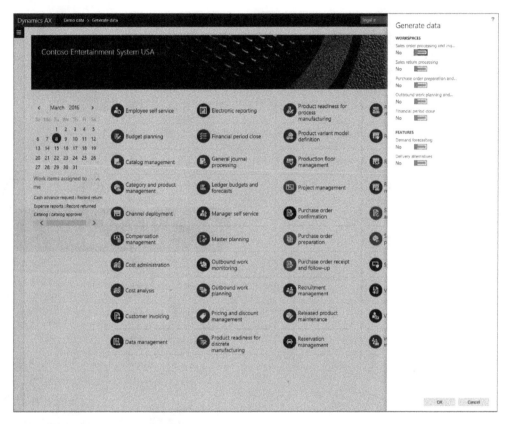

This will open up a dialog panel that shows you all of the different workspaces that you can create the demo data.

Creating demo data

How to do it…

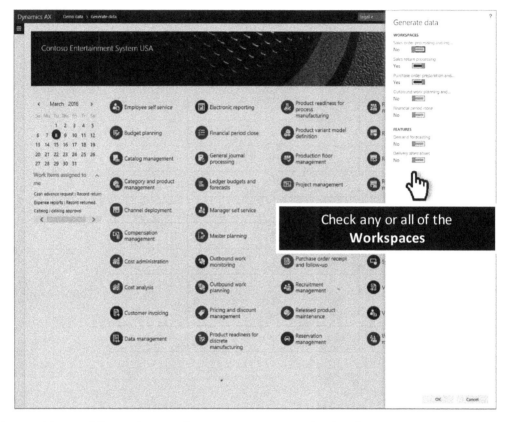

Just enable any of the workspaces that you want to create the data for.

Creating demo data

How to do it…

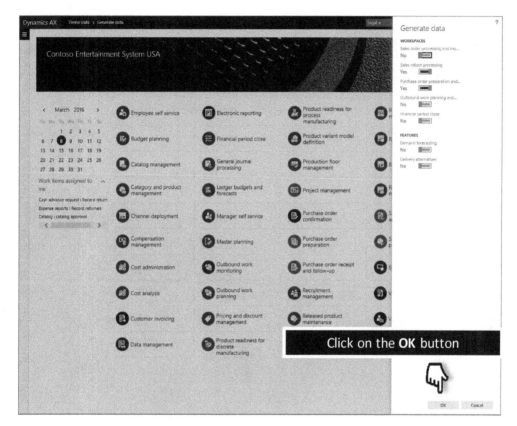

And then click on the OK button to start the demo data creation process.

daxc   www.dynamicsaxcompanions.com
Dynamics AX Companions
- 377 -
www.blindsquirrelpublishing.com
© 2015 Blind Squirrel Publishing, LLC , All Rights Reserved
BLIND SQUIRREL
PUBLISHING

Creating demo data

How to do it…

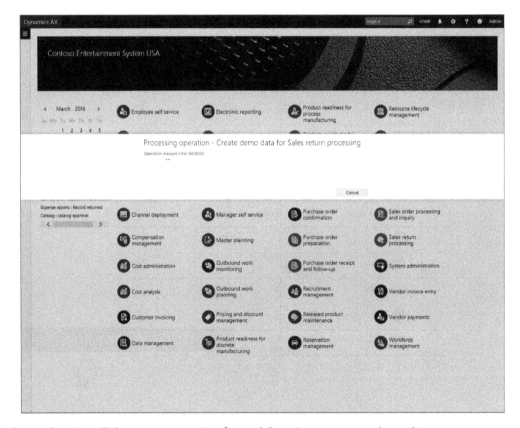

The application will then start processing for a while as it creates your demo data.

It will may also give you some more feedback as it builds additional demo data such as the Financial Period Close data.

Creating demo data

How to do it…

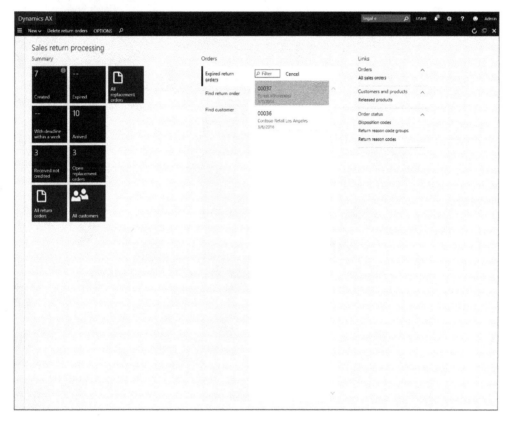

Now when you return to the workspaces you will see that there is demo data associated with the workspaces.

Enabling Power BI

Another key integration point within the new Dynamics AX is the integration with Power BI Online which allows you to generate all of your reporting dashboards within Power BI and then just add them to your workspaces. Before you can do this though you need to first enable them so that they show up on the dashboards.

How to do it...

In order to enable Power BI, start off by pressing ALT+G to go directly to the search box.

Then type in Power Bi to search for the Power BI settings form.

From the list of matching forms select the Power BI menu item from the System Administration group.

This will open up the options for enabling and configuring Power BI.

To change the settings start off by clicking on the Edit button in the menu bar.

That will allow you to edit the fields in the form.

Start off by clicking on the Enabled slider to set it to Yes which will allow the Power BI tile to be displayed.

Then type in the Azure AD Client ID into the Client ID field.

And also the Azure AD Application Key into the Application Key field.

After you have done that then click on the Save button to commit the changes.

Now when you return back to the workspaces – like the Cost Analysis workspace then you will see that there is a new tile that is displayed that shows Power BI.

Enabling Power BI

How to do it…

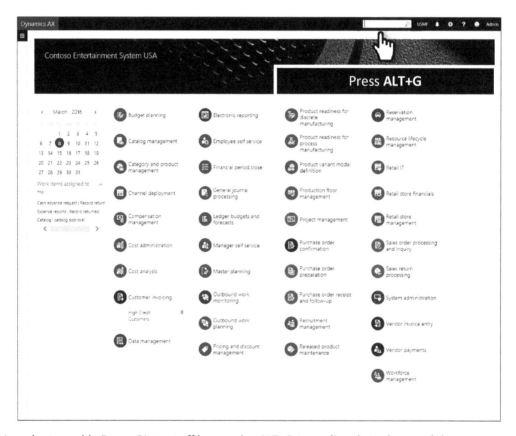

In order to enable Power BI, start off by pressing ALT+G to go directly to the search box.

Enabling Power BI

How to do it...

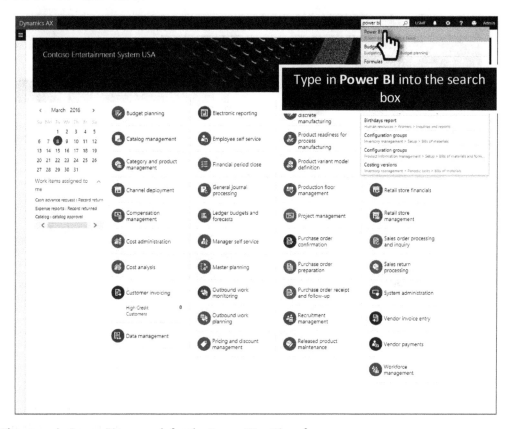

Then type in Power Bi to search for the Power BI settings form.

da✕c www.dynamicsaxcompanions.com
Dynamics AX Companions
- 383 -
www.blindsquirrelpublishing.com
© 2015 Blind Squirrel Publishing, LLC , All Rights Reserved
BLIND SQUIRREL
PUBLISHING

Enabling Power BI

How to do it…

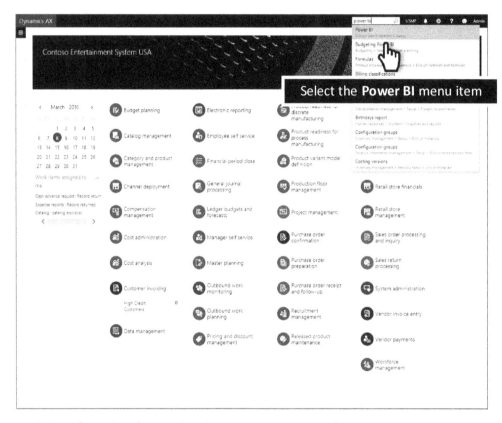

Select the **Power BI** menu item

From the list of matching forms select the Power BI menu item from the System Administration group.

Enabling Power BI

How to do it...

This will open up the options for enabling and configuring Power BI.

Enabling Power BI

How to do it…

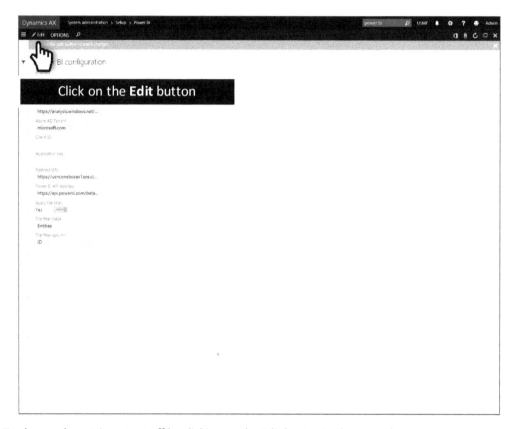

To change the settings start off by clicking on the Edit button in the menu bar.

Enabling Power BI

How to do it...

That will allow you to edit the fields in the form.

 www.dynamicsaxcompanions.com
Dynamics AX Companions

- 387 -

www.blindsquirrelpublishing.com
© 2015 Blind Squirrel Publishing, LLC , All Rights Reserved

BLIND SQUIRREL
PUBLISHING

Enabling Power BI

How to do it…

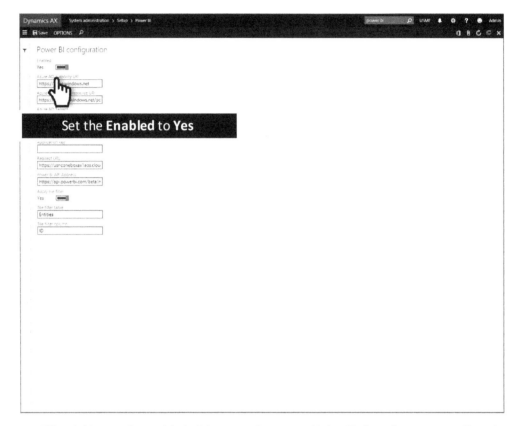

Start off by clicking on the Enabled slider to set it to Yes which will allow the Power BI tile to be displayed.

Enabling Power BI

How to do it…

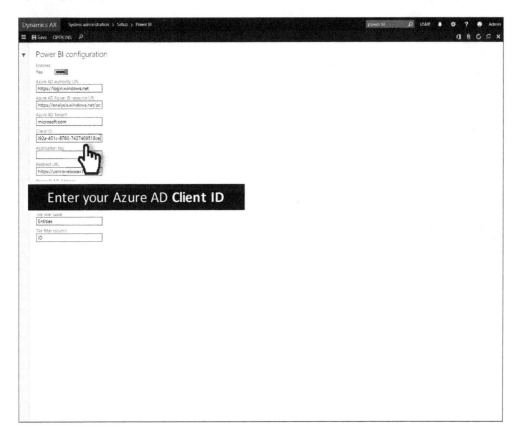

Then type in the Azure AD Client ID into the Client ID field.

Enabling Power BI

How to do it...

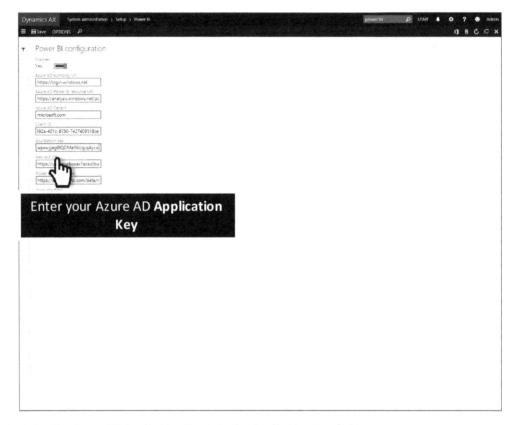

And also the Azure AD Application Key into the Application Key field.

Enabling Power BI

How to do it…

After you have done that then click on the Save button to commit the changes.

dexc www.dynamicsaxcompanions.com
Dynamics AX Companions

- 391 -

www.blindsquirrelpublishing.com
© 2015 Blind Squirrel Publishing, LLC , All Rights Reserved

 BLIND SQUIRREL
PUBLISHING

Enabling Power BI

How to do it…

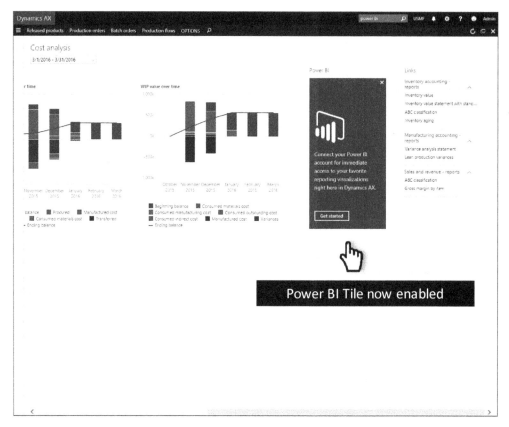

Now when you return back to the workspaces – like the Cost Analysis workspace then you will see that there is a new tile that is displayed that shows Power BI.

da×c   www.dynamicsaxcompanions.com
Dynamics AX Companions
- 392 -
www.blindsquirrelpublishing.com
© 2015 Blind Squirrel Publishing, LLC , All Rights Reserved
BLIND SQUIRREL
PUBLISHING

Connecting to Power BI

Once you have enabled Power BI then the next step that you need to perform is to connect the users account to Power BI so that it will be able to find all of the dashboards that have been published for the user.

How to do it...

To do this, click on the Get Started button.

This will open up an Authorize Power BI dialog box, and all you need to do is click on the Click here to provide authorization to Power BI link.

This will open up a new browser window for you and link the current user account with their Power BI user account. After you get the success notification then you can close down the second browser window.

When you return back, click on the Close button to exit from the Authorization dialog box.

This will then take you to the Add/Remove Power BI tiles dialog box showing you all of the different dashboard components that you can add to your workspace.

Note: if you open up your Power BI application then you will see that all of the Power BI tiles are the same as the ones that are within your users dashboards.

Connecting to Power BI

How to do it…

Click on the **Get Started** button

To do this, click on the Get Started button.

dαxc www.dynamicsaxcompanions.com
Dynamics AX Companions

- 394 -

www.blindsquirrelpublishing.com
© 2015 Blind Squirrel Publishing, LLC , All Rights Reserved

 BLIND SQUIRREL
PUBLISHING

Connecting to Power BI

How to do it...

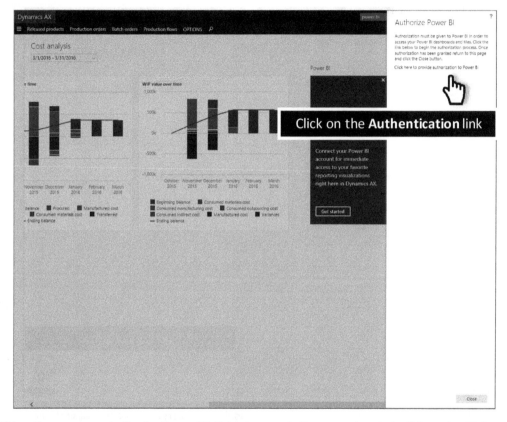

This will open up an Authorize Power BI dialog box, and all you need to do is click on the Click here to provide authorization to Power BI link.

www.dynamicsaxcompanions.com
Dynamics AX Companions

- 395 -

www.blindsquirrelpublishing.com
© 2015 Blind Squirrel Publishing, LLC , All Rights Reserved

BLIND SQUIRREL
PUBLISHING

Connecting to Power BI

How to do it...

This will open up a new browser window for you and link the current user account with their Power BI user account. After you get the success notification then you can close down the second browser window.

daxc   www.dynamicsaxcompanions.com
Dynamics AX Companions
- 396 -
www.blindsquirrelpublishing.com
© 2015 Blind Squirrel Publishing, LLC , All Rights Reserved
BLIND SQUIRREL
PUBLISHING

Connecting to Power BI

How to do it…

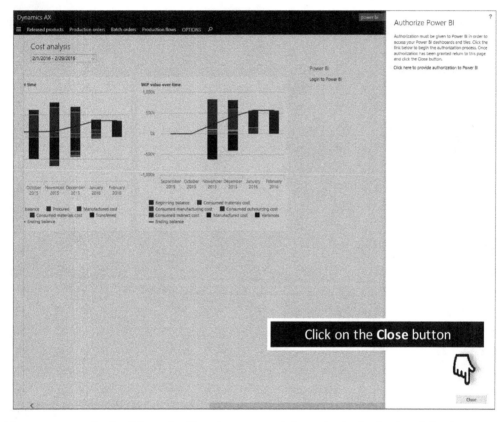

When you return back, click on the Close button to exit from the Authorization dialog box.

daxc www.dynamicsaxcompanions.com
Dynamics AX Companions
- 397 -
www.blindsquirrelpublishing.com
© 2015 Blind Squirrel Publishing, LLC , All Rights Reserved
BLIND SQUIRREL
PUBLISHING

Connecting to Power BI

How to do it…

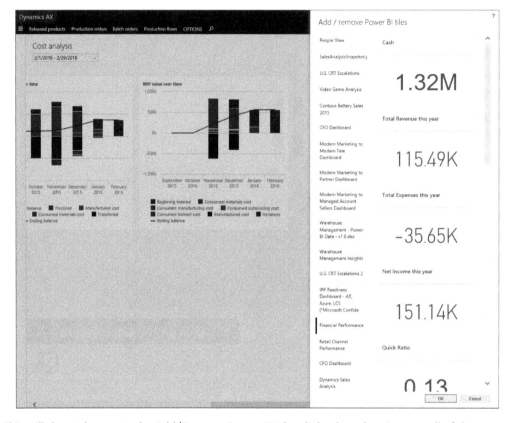

This will then take you to the Add/Remove Power BI tiles dialog box showing you all of the different dashboard components that you can add to your workspace.

daxc   www.dynamicsaxcompanions.com
Dynamics AX Companions
- 398 -
www.blindsquirrelpublishing.com
© 2015 Blind Squirrel Publishing, LLC , All Rights Reserved
BLIND SQUIRREL
PUBLISHING

Connecting to Power BI

How to do it…

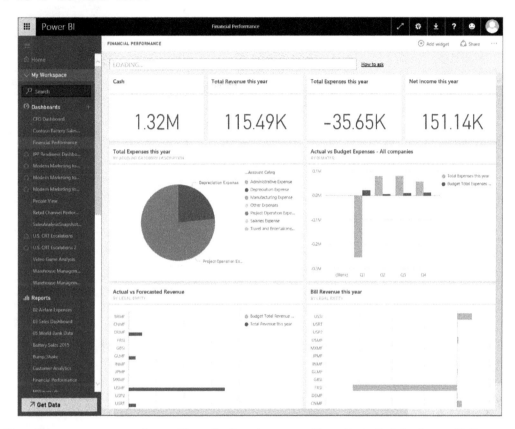

Note: if you open up your Power BI application then you will see that all of the Power BI tiles are the same as the ones that are within your users dashboards.

Adding Power BI tiles to workspaces

Once you have enabled Power BI and linked the account then you can start adding any of the tiles to your workspaces.

How to do it...

To select particular dashboards you can select them from the left hand side of the dialog box.

To add the tiles to the workspace all you need to do is check them.

After you have selected all of the tiles that you want to add then you just need to click on the OK button.

Now you will see that the Power BI tiles have been added to the workspace.

If you want to make changes then you can click on the Add/Remove Power BI Tiles link and repeat the process.

daxc   www.dynamicsaxcompanions.com
Dynamics AX Companions

- 401 -

www.blindsquirrelpublishing.com
© 2015 Blind Squirrel Publishing, LLC , All Rights Reserved

 BLIND SQUIRREL
PUBLISHING

Adding Power BI tiles to workspaces

How to do it...

To select particular dashboards you can select them from the left hand side of the dialog box.

Adding Power BI tiles to workspaces

How to do it...

To add the tiles to the workspace all you need to do is check them.

Adding Power BI tiles to workspaces

How to do it…

After you have selected all of the tiles that you want to add then you just need to click on the OK button.

daxc   www.dynamicsaxcompanions.com
Dynamics AX Companions

- 404 -

www.blindsquirrelpublishing.com
© 2015 Blind Squirrel Publishing, LLC , All Rights Reserved

BLIND SQUIRREL
PUBLISHING

Adding Power BI tiles to workspaces

How to do it…

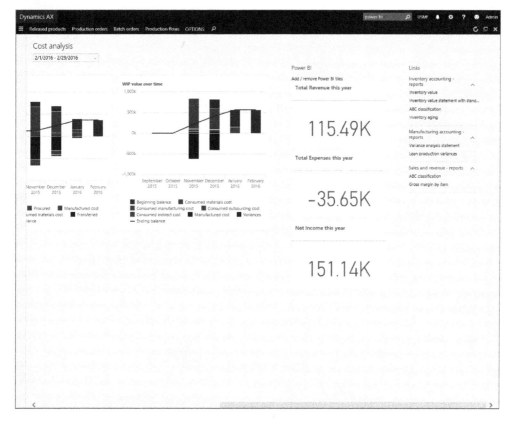

Now you will see that the Power BI tiles have been added to the workspace.

If you want to make changes then you can click on the Add/Remove Power BI Tiles link and repeat the process.

daxc
www.dynamicsaxcompanions.com
Dynamics AX Companions

- 405 -

www.blindsquirrelpublishing.com
© 2015 Blind Squirrel Publishing, LLC , All Rights Reserved

BLIND SQUIRREL
PUBLISHING

Creating a data export template using data management

One of the workspaces that is embedded within the new Dynamics AX is a Data Management workspace. This is a really useful workspace because it allows the user to export data to data packages that can then be used in other environments

How to do it...

To create an export template start off on the default dashboard view and select the Data Management workspace tile.

When the Data management workspace is displayed, click on the Export tile.

This will open up the Export workbench where we will add all of the different items that we want to include within the export template.

Start off by typing in a Name for the export group. In this example we will create a export that has all of the Accounts Receivable codes, so we will set the name to AccountsReceivable.

Next we will want to specify the format for each of the export package files. To do this click on the dropdown list for the Target data format.

da⅋c   www.dynamicsaxcompanions.com
Dynamics AX Companions
- 407 -
www.blindsquirrelpublishing.com
© 2015 Blind Squirrel Publishing, LLC , All Rights Reserved
 BLIND SQUIRREL
PUBLISHING

Here you will see that there are a number of different data format options including CSV formats, AX files, and also Excel. Select the EXCEL data format.

Now we will want to start adding the entities that we want to include within the export package. Rather than search through all of the entities, just type in part of the entity name into the Entity Name field. For example, type in payment sch.

This will give you a list of all of the matching entities including the Payment Schedule entity which you can double click on.

After you have done that then click on the Add entity button.

This will add the entity to your workspace.

You can continue adding in as many other entities into the template as you like.

Creating a data export template using data management

How to do it…

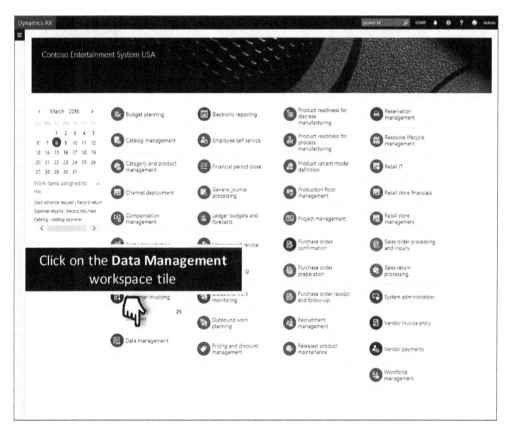

To create an export template start off on the default dashboard view and select the Data Management workspace tile.

www.dynamicsaxcompanions.com
Dynamics AX Companions

- 409 -

www.blindsquirrelpublishing.com
© 2015 Blind Squirrel Publishing, LLC , All Rights Reserved

BLIND SQUIRREL
PUBLISHING

Creating a data export template using data management

How to do it…

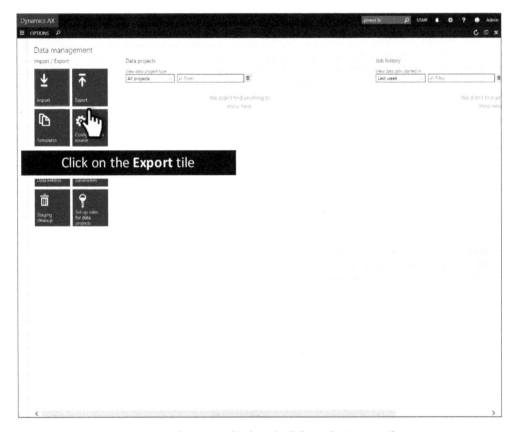

When the Data management workspace is displayed, click on the Export tile.

Creating a data export template using data management

How to do it…

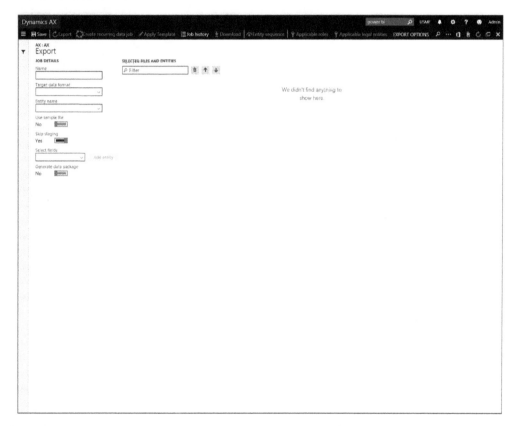

This will open up the Export workbench where we will add all of the different items that we want to include within the export template.

daxc   www.dynamicsaxcompanions.com
Dynamics AX Companions

www.blindsquirrelpublishing.com
© 2015 Blind Squirrel Publishing, LLC , All Rights Reserved

 BLIND SQUIRREL
PUBLISHING

Creating a data export template using data management

How to do it…

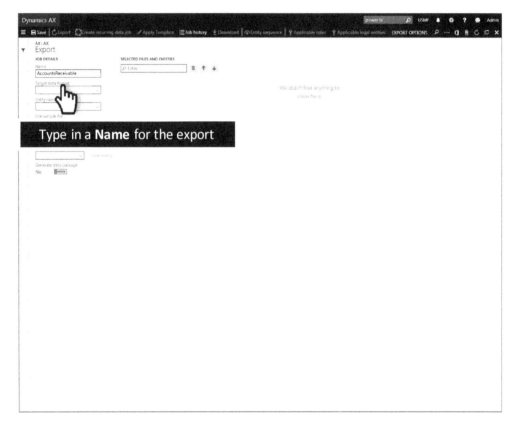

Start off by typing in a Name for the export group. In this example we will create a export that has all of the Accounts Receivable codes, so we will set the name to AccountsReceivable.

da𝔁c www.dynamicsaxcompanions.com
Dynamics AX Companions
- 412 -
www.blindsquirrelpublishing.com
© 2015 Blind Squirrel Publishing, LLC , All Rights Reserved
BLIND SQUIRREL
PUBLISHING

Creating a data export template using data management

How to do it…

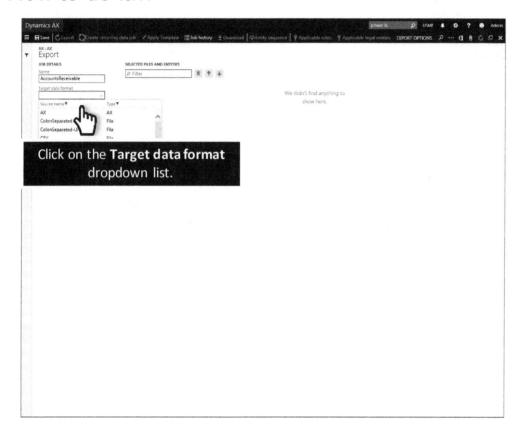

Next we will want to specify the format for each of the export package files. To do this click on the dropdown list for the Target data format.

daxc   www.dynamicsaxcompanions.com
Dynamics AX Companions
- 413 -
www.blindsquirrelpublishing.com
© 2015 Blind Squirrel Publishing, LLC , All Rights Reserved
BLIND SQUIRREL
PUBLISHING

Creating a data export template using data management

How to do it…

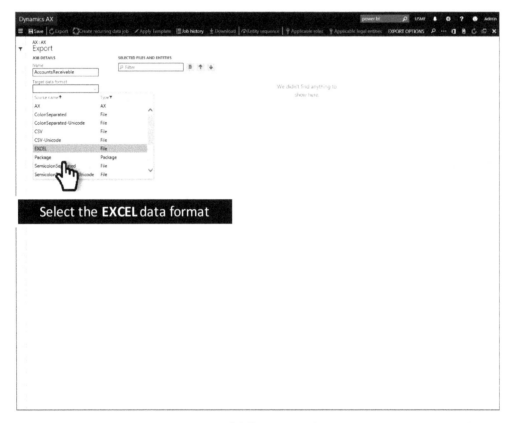

Here you will see that there are a number of different data format options including CSV formats, AX files, and also Excel. Select the EXCEL data format.

www.blindsquirrelpublishing.com
© 2015 Blind Squirrel Publishing, LLC , All Rights Reserved

Creating a data export template using data management

How to do it…

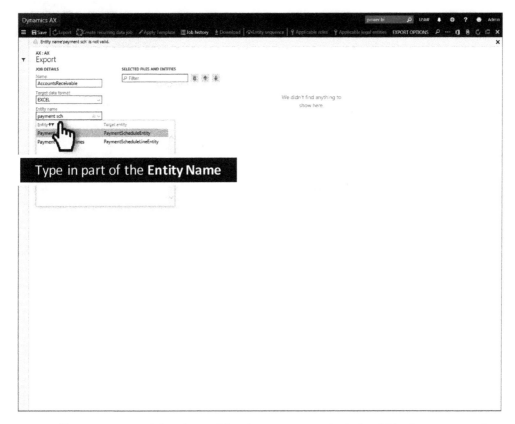

Now we will want to start adding the entities that we want to include within the export package. Rather than search through all of the entities, just type in part of the entity name into the Entity Name field. For example, type in payment sch.

Creating a data export template using data management

How to do it...

This will give you a list of all of the matching entities including the Payment Schedule entity which you can double click on.

daxc   www.dynamicsaxcompanions.com
Dynamics AX Companions
- 416 -
www.blindsquirrelpublishing.com
© 2015 Blind Squirrel Publishing, LLC, All Rights Reserved
BLIND SQUIRREL PUBLISHING

Creating a data export template using data management

How to do it…

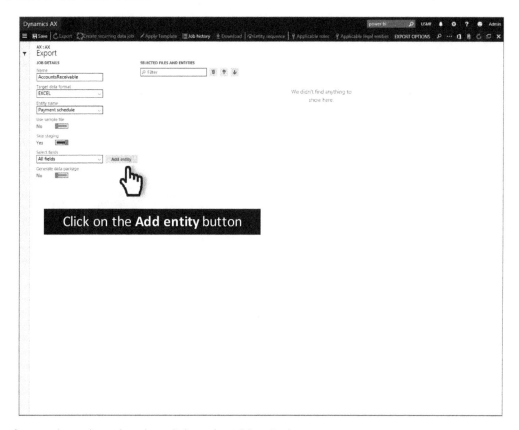

After you have done that then click on the Add entity button.

Creating a data export template using data management

How to do it…

This will add the entity to your workspace.

daxc   www.dynamicsaxcompanions.com
Dynamics AX Companions
- 418 -
www.blindsquirrelpublishing.com
© 2015 Blind Squirrel Publishing, LLC , All Rights Reserved
 BLIND SQUIRREL
PUBLISHING

Creating a data export template using data management

How to do it…

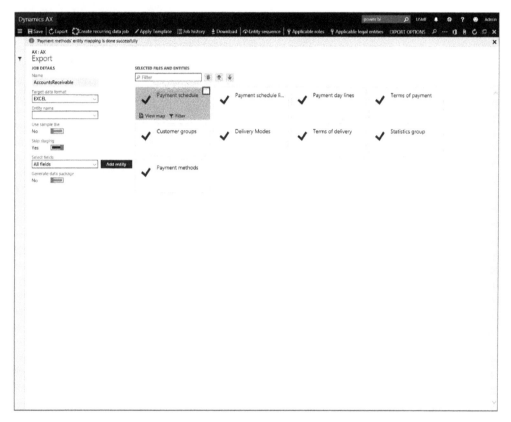

You can continue adding in as many other entities into the template as you like.

daxc www.dynamicsaxcompanions.com
Dynamics AX Companions
- 419 -
www.blindsquirrelpublishing.com
© 2015 Blind Squirrel Publishing, LLC , All Rights Reserved
BLIND SQUIRREL PUBLISHING

Creating a data export

Once you have created the export template it's time to export all of the data.

How to do it...

To do this just click on the Export button in the menu bar.

This will kick off the export process. When the message bar is displayed, click on the Close button.

Now the export will run in the background for you. If you want to see the progress then you may want to click on the Refresh icon in the top right of the form to update your view.

After a bit you will see a summary of all of the records that are created within the export process.

da⅔c   www.dynamicsaxcompanions.com
       Dynamics AX Companions

- 421 -

www.blindsquirrelpublishing.com
© 2015 Blind Squirrel Publishing, LLC , All Rights Reserved

 BLIND SQUIRREL
PUBLISHING

Creating a data export

How to do it...

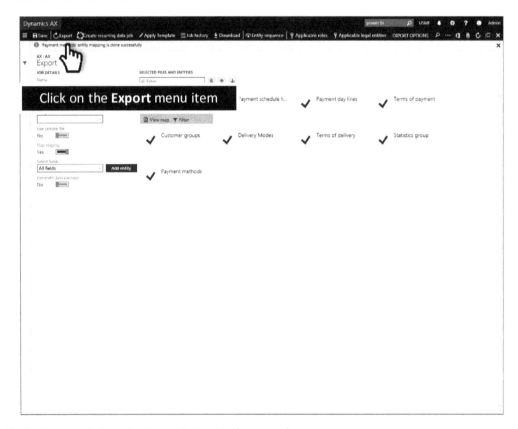

To do this just click on the Export button in the menu bar.

Creating a data export

How to do it…

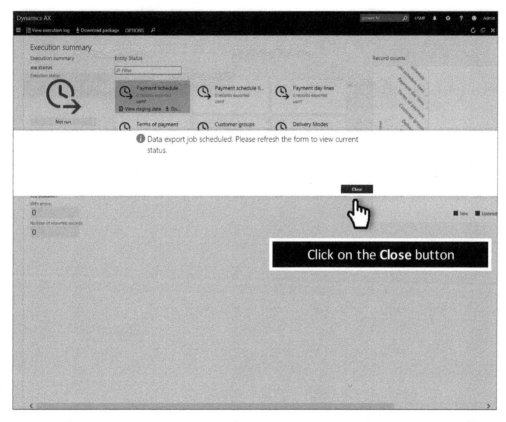

This will kick off the export process. When the message bar is displayed, click on the Close button.

daxc www.dynamicsaxcompanions.com
Dynamics AX Companions
- 423 -
www.blindsquirrelpublishing.com
© 2015 Blind Squirrel Publishing, LLC , All Rights Reserved

BLIND SQUIRREL
PUBLISHING

Creating a data export

How to do it…

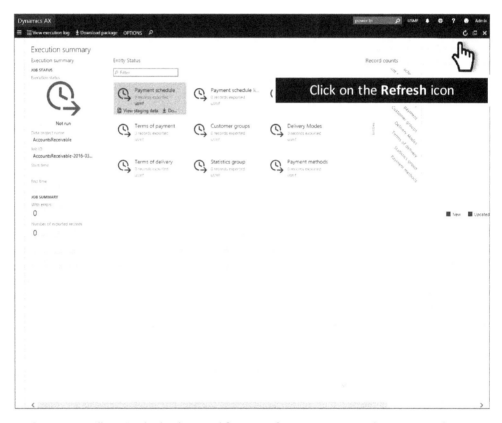

Now the export will run in the background for you. If you want to see the progress then you may want to click on the Refresh icon in the top right of the form to update your view.

daxc   www.dynamicsaxcompanions.com
Dynamics AX Companions

- 424 -

www.blindsquirrelpublishing.com
© 2015 Blind Squirrel Publishing, LLC , All Rights Reserved

BLIND SQUIRREL
PUBLISHING

Creating a data export

How to do it...

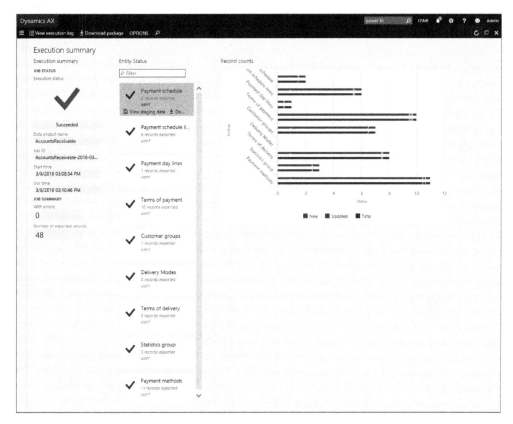

After a bit you will see a summary of all of the records that are created within the export process.

Downloading your data to a package

Once you have created the export, you can then save it off as a data package. This has a number of benefits because the package is then a local file that you can share, edit, and also use within other systems.

How to do it...

To do this, just click on the Download package menu item.

When the message is displayed saying that there is no data package, and do you want to create one click on the Yes button.

This will create the data package for you and all you need to do is file it away. So when the file options bar is displayed, click on the Save options and then select the Save as menu item.

This will open up a Save As dialog box.

The file name is a little cryptic as a GUID so change the file name to something a little more understandable like AccountsReceivable_DataPackage.

And then click on the Save button.

This will save the file and open it up for you. It is really just a zip file with all of the data saved away in individual Excel worksheets. Click on the Customer groups file – or any other one that you like.

You will see that the file is a spreadsheet with all of the columns from Dynamics AX and a row for each piece of data.

Downloading your data to a package

How to do it...

To do this, just click on the Download package menu item.

Downloading your data to a package

How to do it...

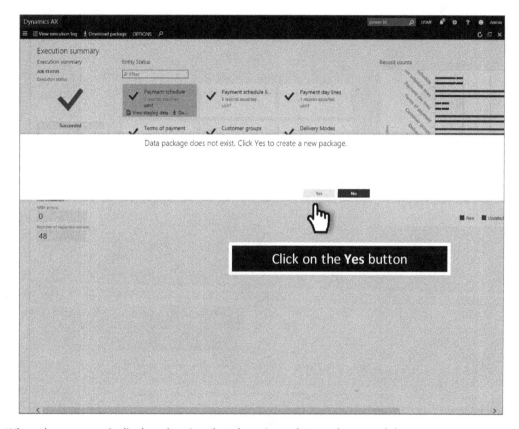

When the message is displayed saying that there is no data package, and do you want to create one click on the Yes button.

Downloading your data to a package

How to do it...

This will create the data package for you and all you need to do is file it away. So when the file options bar is displayed, click on the Save options and then select the Save as menu item.

daxc   www.dynamicsaxcompanions.com
Dynamics AX Companions

- 430 -

www.blindsquirrelpublishing.com
© 2015 Blind Squirrel Publishing, LLC , All Rights Reserved

BLIND SQUIRREL
PUBLISHING

Downloading your data to a package

How to do it...

This will open up a Save As dialog box.

Downloading your data to a package

How to do it…

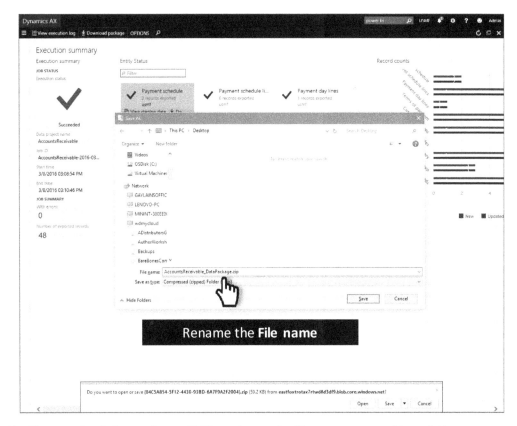

Rename the **File name**

The file name is a little cryptic as a GUID so change the file name to something a little more understandable like AccountsReceivable_DataPackage.

daxc   www.dynamicsaxcompanions.com
Dynamics AX Companions
- 432 -
www.blindsquirrelpublishing.com
© 2015 Blind Squirrel Publishing, LLC , All Rights Reserved
BLIND SQUIRREL PUBLISHING

Downloading your data to a package

How to do it...

And then click on the Save button.

Downloading your data to a package

How to do it...

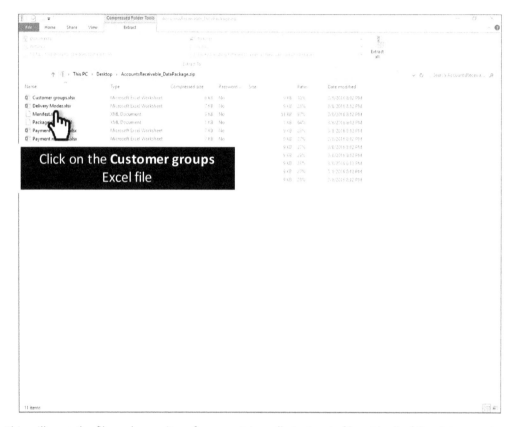

Click on the **Customer groups** Excel file

This will save the file and open it up for you. It is really just a zip file with all of the data saved away in individual Excel worksheets. Click on the Customer groups file – or any other one that you like.

Downloading your data to a package

How to do it...

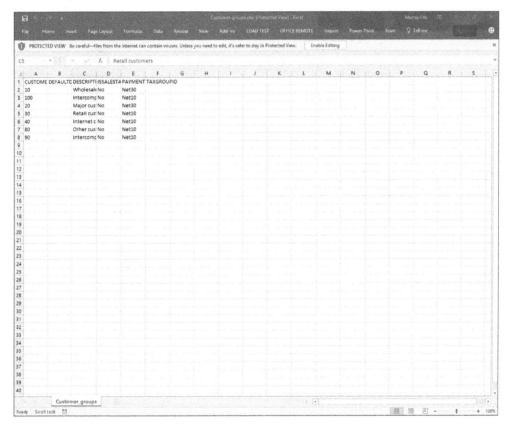

You will see that the file is a spreadsheet with all of the columns from Dynamics AX and a row for each piece of data.

Importing data packages into other entities

Once you have created the export packages then you can use them to hydrate other instances of Dynamics Ax and even other new Legal Entities that you may be creating. This is definitely a great way to create reusable data import templates.

How to do it...

To do this switch to the environment or legal entity that you want to import the data package and then click on the Data Management workspace tile within the default dashboard.

When the Data Management workspace is displayed, click on the Import tile.

This will open up the data Import workbench.

The first thing we need to do is enter in a Name for the import project.

Then click on the Source data format dropdown list to show all of the different options that we have as the source data.

Since we created a package with our data in it select the Package option.

Then click on the Upload button.

 BLIND SQUIRREL PUBLISHING

This will open up a file explorer and you just need to browse to the location of the data export package and then click on the Open button.

This will start off a import function which will examine the manifest of the package and find all of the data entities that are in there.

Within a couple of seconds the import project will get populated with all of the entities that were included in the file.

To start the import process, just click on the Import menu item in the menu bar.

This will then kick off the import as a background process. When the message bar is displayed, click on the Close button.

As the process runs you will be able to see all of the data as it's being loaded. If you want you can click on the Refresh icon in the top right hand corner of the application to track the progress.

After just a bit you will see all of the data that has been imported and if there are any quirks in the data that is being loaded.

When the form is displayed you will see that all of the Terms of Payments are now populated and loaded into the blank entity.

daxc
www.dynamicsaxcompanions.com
Dynamics AX Companions

- 438 -

www.blindsquirrelpublishing.com
© 2015 Blind Squirrel Publishing, LLC , All Rights Reserved

BLIND SQUIRREL
PUBLISHING

Importing data packages into other entities

How to do it…

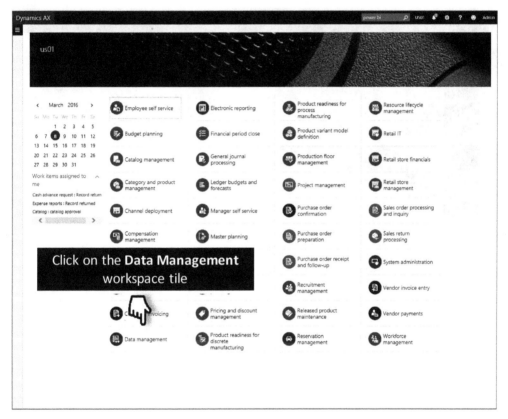

To do this switch to the environment or legal entity that you want to import the data package and then click on the Data Management workspace tile within the default dashboard.

Importing data packages into other entities

How to do it…

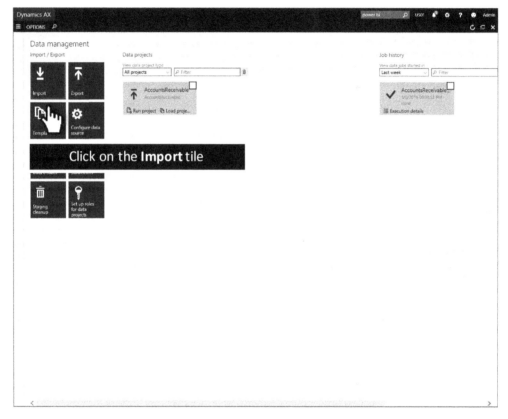

When the Data Management workspace is displayed, click on the Import tile.

Importing data packages into other entities

How to do it…

This will open up the data Import workbench.

www.dynamicsaxcompanions.com
Dynamics AX Companions

- 441 -

www.blindsquirrelpublishing.com
© 2015 Blind Squirrel Publishing, LLC , All Rights Reserved

BLIND SQUIRREL
PUBLISHING

Importing data packages into other entities

How to do it…

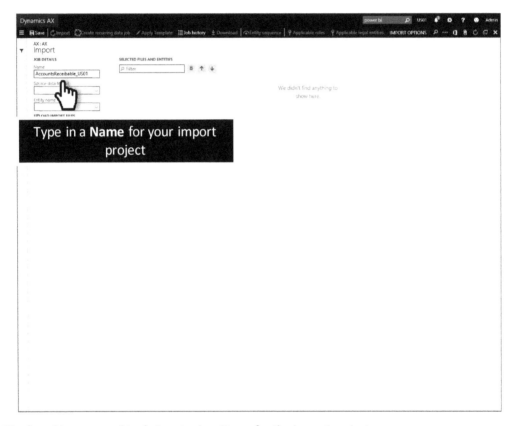

The first thing we need to do is enter in a Name for the import project.

Importing data packages into other entities

How to do it...

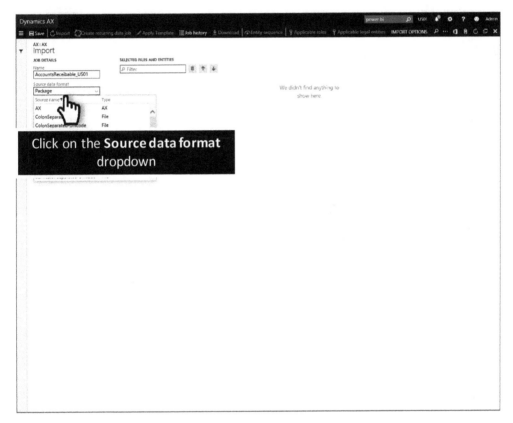

Then click on the Source data format dropdown list to show all of the different options that we have as the source data.

daxc www.dynamicsaxcompanions.com
Dynamics AX Companions

- 443 -

www.blindsquirrelpublishing.com
© 2015 Blind Squirrel Publishing, LLC , All Rights Reserved

BLIND SQUIRREL
PUBLISHING

Importing data packages into other entities

How to do it…

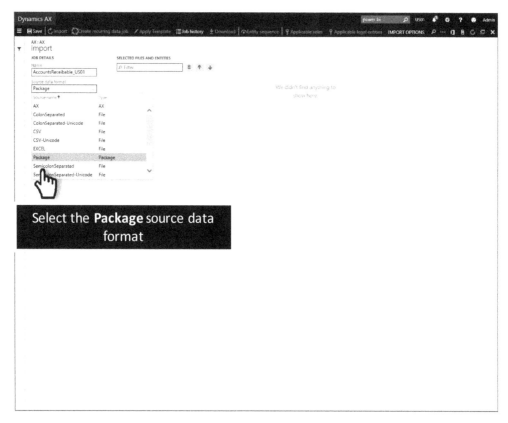

Select the **Package** source data format

Since we created a package with our data in it select the Package option.

daxc www.dynamicsaxcompanions.com
Dynamics AX Companions
- 444 -
www.blindsquirrelpublishing.com
© 2015 Blind Squirrel Publishing, LLC , All Rights Reserved

BLIND SQUIRREL
PUBLISHING

Importing data packages into other entities

How to do it...

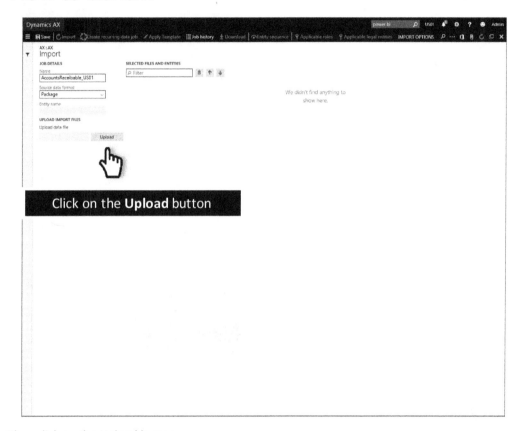

Then click on the Upload button.

Importing data packages into other entities

How to do it…

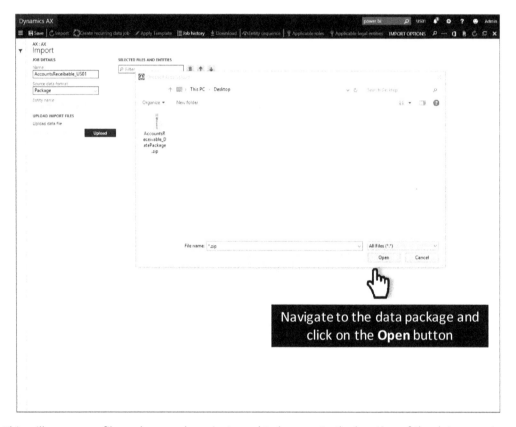

Navigate to the data package and click on the **Open** button

This will open up a file explorer and you just need to browse to the location of the data export package and then click on the Open button.

da&c www.dynamicsaxcompanions.com
Dynamics AX Companions
- 446 -
www.blindsquirrelpublishing.com
© 2015 Blind Squirrel Publishing, LLC , All Rights Reserved
 BLIND SQUIRREL PUBLISHING

Importing data packages into other entities

How to do it…

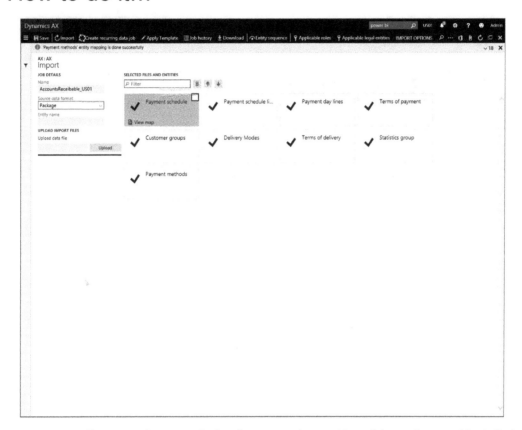

This will start off a import function which will examine the manifest of the package and find all of the data entities that are in there.

Within a couple of seconds the import project will get populated with all of the entities that were included in the file.

da×c   www.dynamicsaxcompanions.com
        Dynamics AX Companions

- 447 -

www.blindsquirrelpublishing.com
© 2015 Blind Squirrel Publishing, LLC , All Rights Reserved

BLIND SQUIRREL
PUBLISHING

Importing data packages into other entities

How to do it…

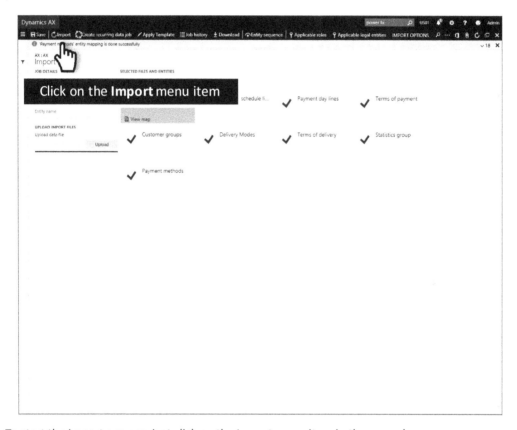

To start the import process, just click on the Import menu item in the menu bar.

da<c   www.dynamicsaxcompanions.com
Dynamics AX Companions
- 448 -
www.blindsquirrelpublishing.com
© 2015 Blind Squirrel Publishing, LLC , All Rights Reserved
 BLIND SQUIRREL PUBLISHING

Importing data packages into other entities

How to do it...

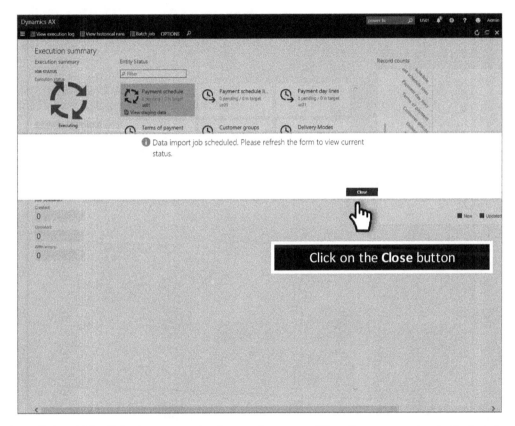

This will then kick off the import as a background process. When the message bar is displayed, click on the Close button.

Importing data packages into other entities

How to do it…

As the process runs you will be able to see all of the data as it's being loaded. If you want you can click on the Refresh icon in the top right hand corner of the application to track the progress.

Importing data packages into other entities

How to do it…

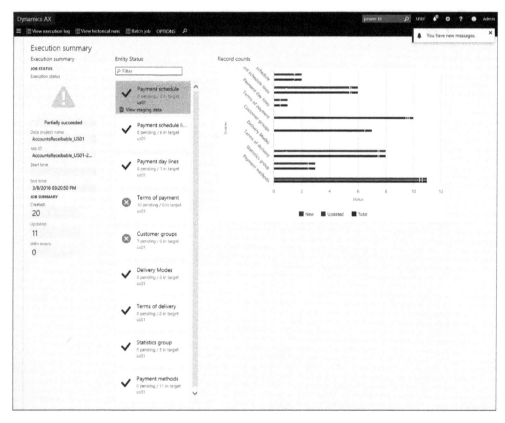

After just a bit you will see all of the data that has been imported and if there are any quirks in the data that is being loaded.

Importing data packages into other entities

How to do it…

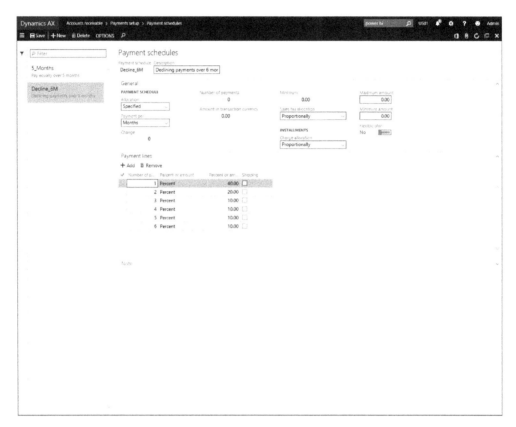

When the form is displayed you will see that all of the Terms of Payments are now populated and loaded into the blank entity.

daxc   www.dynamicsaxcompanions.com
        Dynamics AX Companions

- 452 -

www.blindsquirrelpublishing.com
© 2015 Blind Squirrel Publishing, LLC , All Rights Reserved

BLIND SQUIRREL
PUBLISHING

CONCLUSION

Hopefully this guide has given you all a little better idea of some of the features within the new Dynamics AX system and also taught you a couple of tricks that you didn't already know about, and also a couple of tricks that will help you as you are learning to navigate through the new user interface. We are not pretending that these are the only features that are hidden away within the system and as we learn more we will definitely be sharing those with you all as well.

In the meantime, we think this a good start.

 www.dynamicsaxcompanions.com
Dynamics AX Companions

- 453 -

www.blindsquirrelpublishing.com
© 2015 Blind Squirrel Publishing, LLC , All Rights Reserved

 BLIND SQUIRREL
PUBLISHING

About The Author

Murray Fife is an Author of over 20 books on Microsoft Dynamics AX including the Bare Bones Configuration Guide series of over 15 books which step the user through the setup of initial Dynamics AX instance, then through the Financial modules and then through the configuration of the more specialized modules like production, service management, and project accounting. You can find all of his books on Amazon (www.amazon.com/author/murrayfife) and also even more on the BSP (www.blindsquirrelpublishing.com) site.

Murray is also the curator of the Dynamics AX Companions (www.dynamicsaxcompanions.com) site which he built from the ground up as a resource for all of the Dynamics AX community where you can find walkthroughs and blueprints that he created since first being introduced to the Dynamics AX product.

Throughout his 25+ years of experience in the software industry he has worked in many different roles during his career, including as a developer, an implementation consultant, a trainer and a demo guy within the partner channel which gives him a great understanding of the requirements for both customers and partner's perspective.

He is also a great supporter of the Dynamics AX community and has hosted scores webinars for the AX User Group (www.axug.com) and MS Dynamics World (www.msdynamicsworld.com), and has spoken at Microsoft Convergence and AXUG Summit conferences more times than he can count.

For more information on Murray, here is his contact information:

Email:	murrayfife@dynamicsaxcompanions.com
Twitter:	@murrayfife
Facebook:	facebook.com/murraycfife
Google:	google.com/+murrayfife
LinkedIn:	linkedin.com/in/murrayfife
Blog:	atinkerersnotebook.com
Docs:	docs.com/mufife
Amazon:	amazon.com/author/murrayfife

Need More Help With Dynamics AX

The Bare Bones Configuration Guides for Dynamics AX was developed to show you how to set up a company from the ground up and configure all of the common modules that most people would need, and a few that you might want to use.

It aims to demystify the setup process and prove that Dynamics AX is only as hard to configure as you make it, and if you are a mid-range customer that even you can get a company configured and working without turning on every bell and whistle and without breaking the bank.

There are 16 volumes in the current series and although each of these guides have been designed to stand by themselves as reference material for each of the modules within Dynamics AX, if they are taken as a whole series they are also a great training system that will allow even a novice on Dynamics AX work through the step by step instructions and build up a new company from scratch and learn a lot of the ins and outs of the system right away. The current guides are:

1. Configuring a Base Dynamics AX 2012 System
2. Configuring an Organization Within Dynamics AX 2012
3. Configuring The General Ledger Within Dynamics AX 2012
4. Configuring Cash And Bank Management Within Dynamics AX 2012
5. Configuring Accounts Receivable Within Dynamics AX 2012
6. Configuring Accounts Payable Within Dynamics AX 2012
7. Configuring Product Information Management Within Dynamics AX 2012
8. Configuring Inventory Management Within Dynamics AX 2012
9. Configuring Procurement & Sourcing Within Dynamics AX 2012
10. Configuring Sales Order Management Within Dynamics AX 2012
11. Configuring Human Resources Within Dynamics AX 2012
12. Configuring Project Management & Accounting Within Dynamics AX 2012
13. Configuring Production Control Within Dynamics AX 2012
14. Configuring Sales & Marketing Within Dynamics AX 2012

15. Configuring Service Management Within Dynamics AX 2012
18. Configuring Warehouse Management Within Dynamics AX 2012

If you are interested in finding out more about the series and also view all of the details including topics covered within the module then browse to the Bare Bones Configuration Guide landing page on the Dynamics AX Companions website. You will find all of the details, and also downloadable resources that help you with the setup of Dynamics AX. If you decipher the code in the signature at the bottom of this email then you can get 20% off the books. Here is the full link:

http://www.dynamicsaxcompanions.com/barebonesconfig

Usage Agreement

Murray Fife (the Author) agrees to grant, and the user of the eBook agrees to accept, a nonexclusive license to use the eBook under the terms and conditions of this eBook License Agreement ("Agreement"). Your use of the eBook constitutes your agreement to the terms and conditions set forth in this Agreement. This Agreement, or any part thereof, cannot be changed, waived, or discharged other than by a statement in writing signed by you and Murray Fife. Please read the entire Agreement carefully.

1. EBook Usage. The eBook may be used by one user on any device. The user of the eBook shall be subject to all of the terms of this Agreement, whether or not the user was the purchaser.

2. Printing. You may occasionally print a few pages of the eBook's text (but not entire sections), which may include sending the printed pages to a third party in the normal course of your business, but you must warn the recipient in writing that copyright law prohibits the recipient from redistributing the eBook content to anyone else. Other than the above, you may not print pages and/or distribute eBook content to others.

3. Copyright, Use and Resale Prohibitions. The Author retains all rights not expressly granted to you in this Agreement. The software, content, and related documentation in the eBook are protected by copyright laws and international copyright treaties, as well as other intellectual property laws and treaties. Nothing in this Agreement constitutes a waiver of the author's rights. The Author will not be responsible for performance problems due to circumstances beyond its reasonable control. Other than as stated in this Agreement, you may not copy, print, modify, remove, delete, augment, add to, publish, transmit, sell, resell, license, create derivative works from, or in any way exploit any of the eBook's content, in whole or in part, in print or electronic form, and you may not aid or permit others to do so. The unauthorized use or distribution of copyrighted or other proprietary content is illegal and could subject the purchaser to substantial damages. Purchaser will be liable for any damage resulting from any violation of this Agreement.

4. No Transfer. This license is not transferable by the eBook purchaser unless such transfer is approved in advance by the Author.

5. Disclaimer. The eBook, or any support given by the Author are in no way substitutes for assistance from legal, tax, accounting, or other qualified professionals. If legal advice or other expert assistance is required, the services of a competent professional person should be sought.

6. Limitation of Liability. The eBook is provided "as is" and the Author does not make any warranty or representation, either express or implied, to the eBook, including its quality, accuracy, performance, merchantability, or fitness for a particular purpose. You assume the entire risk as to the results and performance of the eBook. The Author does not warrant, guarantee, or make any representations regarding the use of, or the results obtained with, the eBook in terms of accuracy, correctness or reliability. In no event will the Author be liable for indirect, special, incidental, or consequential damages arising out of delays, errors, omissions, inaccuracies, or the use or inability to use the eBook, or for interruption of the eBook, from whatever cause. This will apply even if the Author has been advised that the possibility of such damage exists. Specifically, the Author is not responsible for any costs, including those incurred as a result of lost profits or revenue, loss of data, the cost of recovering such programs or data, the cost of any substitute program, claims by third parties, or similar costs. Except for the Author's indemnification obligations in Section 7.2, in no case will the Author's liability exceed the amount of license fees paid.

7. Hold Harmless / Indemnification.
7.1 You agree to defend, indemnify and hold the Author and any third party provider harmless from and against all third party claims and damages (including reasonable attorneys' fees) regarding your use of the eBook, unless the claims or damages are due to the Author's or any third party provider's gross negligence or willful misconduct or arise out of an allegation for which the Author is obligated to indemnify you.

7.2. The Author shall defend, indemnify and hold you harmless at the Author's expense in any suit, claim or proceeding brought against you alleging that your use of the eBook delivered to you hereunder directly infringes a United States patent, copyright, trademark, trade secret, or other third party proprietary right, provided the Author is (i) promptly notified, (ii) given the assistance required at the Author's expense, and (iii) permitted to retain legal counsel of the Author's choice and to direct the defense. The Author also agrees to pay any damages and costs awarded against you by final judgment of a court of last resort in any such suit or any agreed settlement amount on account of any such alleged infringement, but the Author will have no liability for settlements or costs incurred without its consent. Should your use of any such eBook be enjoined, or in the event that the Author desires to minimize its liability hereunder, the Author will, at its option and expense, (i) substitute a fully equivalent non-infringing eBook for the infringing item; (ii) modify the infringing item so that it no longer infringes but remains substantially equivalent; or (iii) obtain for you the right to continue use of such item. If none of the foregoing is feasible, the Author will terminate your access to the eBook and refund to you the applicable fees paid by you for the infringing item(s). THE FOREGOING STATES THE ENTIRE LIABILITY OF THE AUTHOR AND YOUR SOLE REMEDY FOR INFRINGEMENT OR FOR ANY BREACH OF WARRANTY OF NON-INFRINGEMENT, EXPRESS OR IMPLIED. THIS INDEMNITY WILL NOT APPLY TO ANY ALLEGED INFRINGEMENT BASED UPON A COMBINATION OF OTHER SOFTWARE OR INFORMATION WITH THE EBOOK WHERE THE EBOOK WOULD NOT HAVE OTHERWISE INFRINGED ON ITS OWN.